EMBATTLED JUSTICE

EMBATTLED JUSTICE

T H E S T O R Y O F
LOUIS DEMBITZ BRANDEIS

by ELLEN NORMAN STERN

THE JEWISH PUBLICATION SOCIETY OF AMERICA
PHILADELPHIA   5731 / 1971

With the exception of Dave, who is an invention of the author, all persons named were living people who played a part in the story of Justice Brandeis.

For my husband, Harold,
whose idea it was to write the story of
Justice Louis D. Brandeis

PREFACE

The portico of the Law School Building of the University of Louisville serves as the final resting-place for Justice Louis D. Brandeis and his wife.

During my student days at the university, I passed this site almost daily. It is difficult to escape the spirit which surrounds this spot with special magic.

It is a spirit that has no limitations. As I traveled out into the world, away from Louisville, I discovered that the ideals and hopes which had motivated Justice Brandeis to work for "a decent life" for all people are not confined to the briefs and opinions filed in the room of the law school dedicated to his memory.

The work of Louis D. Brandeis has become a living part of his country's heritage, accepted and taken for granted. Yet many of the privileges which we now consider a normal part of our American way of life would never have become reality had it not been for the perseverance and steady labors of Justice Brandeis.

May his spirit of persistence in the struggle against indifference and overwhelming opposition serve as an inspiration.

EMBATTLED JUSTICE

ONE

"Louis, Louis. Come down right away. Mamma needs us."

It was his brother, Alfred, calling from the bottom of the steps. Louis was deep in thought, memorizing the lines of Papa's birthday poem. Now seven years old, he was the youngest child in the family. He always recited the verses written by his older sisters for these family occasions. He learned quickly. Fanny or Amy read his lines to him a few times, just to get the right shading into them, and then they stayed in his mind. He had entered school last year and had started reading; it wouldn't be long before he would compose his own poems.

"Louis, hurry. The soldiers are here again."

Many times during the long winter Alfred or one of the girls had called to him, and he had run out to help Mamma and the other children hand out the hot coffee and the good biscuits Cook made right in their kitchen to the soldiers who passed the Brandeis house on their way south.

Louis had been sitting on his bed, his long legs hunched up, reciting his lines. His deep-set dark eyes were closed in concentration. Now he jumped up and looked out the window of the front bedroom he shared with Alfred. Below, just turning the corner from Walnut into First Street, a troop of Union foot soldiers marched toward them. Through the tops of the trees he glimpsed Mamma, Fanny, and Amy setting up their little table on the sidewalk.

It was May 1863 in Louisville—wartime.

In Kentucky springs were warm. He was sure these weary, dusty fellows could use the cool drinks of lemonade awaiting them.

As Louis skipped down the center staircase on his way outside, it seemed to him it had always been wartime and that he had seen soldiers march past their house on First Street all his life.

Louis David Brandeis was born in Louisville in 1856. Louisville was a river town and an exciting place in which to grow up. Louis loved the river and wanted to be near it as often as he could. Steamboats sailed their cargoes of goods between New Orleans and Louisville. How exciting it was to stand on the docks and watch the unloading of riverboats—the sights and sounds of the Ohio River thrilled Louis and Alfred. They loved to go swimming in it as well. On many a summer afternoon they would frolic in the water near Shippingport by the falls of the Ohio. From there the boys could see incoming steamers transfer their loads and passengers, for this was as far as ships could approach without danger of becoming stranded in shallow water. What fun it was to observe the debarkation of the fashionable ladies and gentlemen who had come to Louisville for a summer visit.

But there was a special thrill to their riverwatching which they shared with the whole family: when the *Fanny Brandeis* sailed past them on her way north, loaded with the white wheat ground in the family mill, the boys' joy became almost unbearable. Papa's firm now owned a river freighter, named after Louis's oldest sister, which carried their merchandise as far as New York. There, Kentucky wheat was a prized commodity, especially during these war years when trade with the southern states was cut off.

Papa was doing well now. Despite the war, his grain and produce business prospered. Kentucky was a slave state but had tried to remain neutral in the conflict between the states, allowing her merchants to trade with both the North and South and sending troops to both sides.

Though business was good, it was a difficult time for everybody. Not only were there soldiers constantly in the streets, but several times fighting had broken out within the state's borders. Once they actually heard the sounds of guns as rebel forces closed in on the city. Papa had come home hurriedly that day, loaded them into the carriage, and driven them across the river into Indiana until all was quiet again in Louisville.

Louis thought a lot about the war. Tempers flared easily among grown-ups when they talked about it. How divided their opinions were. Though he was very young, to Louis it seemed that no one group of people had the right to control the lives of others simply because one group had been born white and the other black. Of course, he knew that his family were abolitionists. They were opposed to slavery and thought it wrong for people to keep slaves and exploit them.

Papa and Uncle Lewis N. Dembitz—Mamma's brother—often discussed their views at the dinner table, even in front of the children. Sometimes they switched to their native German if they didn't want the servants to hear. It was a risky time.

Many of the neighbors, and some of their friends, too, did not think like the Brandeises. People who did not like them, or people who envied Papa's success in business, even said nasty things about them, mean things like: "Those foreigners, who do they think they are! Why didn't they stay where they belong, instead of coming over here to make trouble?"

Louis remembered the day last January when President Lincoln's Emancipation Proclamation had been published in the newspaper. Handbills had been posted in the streets. There was much ugly sentiment in the city, but the Brandeis house was filled with happy excitement.

"Greatest document of the century," Uncle Lewis had called it.

"We must celebrate," Mamma had said. "This is a monumental step toward freedom for all people." She even brought out a bottle of imported wine to have with their dinner.

Mamma had read the whole statement to all four

children and explained that from now on most slaves in America were to be freed. "It's a wonderful thing that's happening," she said over and over.

Louis knew it was an unusual day because after dinner he was allowed to stay up beyond his bedtime and had sat in the parlor listening to the adults.

Freedom. Was there ever a family which prized the meaning of the word more? Louis was now old enough to be told about the search for freedom which had brought his whole family over from Europe fourteen years earlier.

Sometimes when Papa was in a relaxed mood and had time to sit down with all the children around him, Louis asked questions about life in the Old World.

"Were you in danger, Papa? Did you come here because you are Jewish?"

And then Papa explained how in Central Europe in 1848 a series of revolutions was going on. It wasn't religious persecution alone which made people leave. But it was a period of general unrest and dissatisfaction. Old political ideas had kept much of Europe suppressed for centuries.

"When our ideas of freedom did not work out the way we had hoped, many of us, still young and adventurous, looked toward America to fulfill our dreams."

Louis loved to hear the story of his father's scouting trip to America. He had been sent ahead to investigate the country and had traveled and worked his way through Pennsylvania and Ohio before deciding to settle the clan in Madison, Indiana. And a clan it was: there were twenty-seven Brandeises, including the members of his mother's family, the Dembitzes and Wehles, who had left Bohemia together and traveled in one boatload aboard the S. S. *Washington* that April of 1849.

Papa and Mamma were only engaged at the time. After their marriage, the start of their life together was also a new start in a new country. Adolph Brandeis, Louis's father, had rented a four-story house in Madison, and there Adolph and Frederika Brandeis began their own little community, in the company of brothers, in-laws, and cousins. Their lives centered around the produce store that Adolph opened. The family had great hopes of doing well in Madison. But business did not turn out as favorably as they had hoped, and within two years the family split up. Some of them moved to New York, one branch went to Cincinnati, and Louis's parents and their oldest child, Fanny, settled in nearby Louisville, just across the Ohio River.

Summers were filled with fun and the outdoors for the Brandeis children. In the family stable there were always horses ready for business use, but many times they were also available for Louis and Alfred to ride. The boys were always happy to be near horses. Living in a part of the country where horses were valued, they learned to ride early and kept their love for this sport the greater part of their lives.

Once during the war a black gelding, a favorite of the whole family, was stolen right out of the stable. A search was made throughout the neighborhood; Papa offered a reward. But the horse was not found. The boys grieved for it a long time and remembered their pet for many years.

On warm summer evenings the family took rides along the River Road and allowed the gentle breezes blowing in from the water to cool them off and ease their weariness from the heat. As the sun disappeared across the river, it was pleasant to speculate about the world spread out beyond and plan the trips and vacations which were to take them away from Louisville. The children knew they were fortunate. Their father was able to send them east even during the war. What an adventure it was to take the railroad all the way up to New York for a visit with their mother's family there. How lucky they were to have those wonderful days in Newport. There they could enjoy all the water sports they loved and on long, lazy afternoons visit among all their uncles, aunts, and cousins who had also come there on vacation.

What a different sort of adventure awaited them in fall and wintertime.

Louis loved school right from the beginning. In Mr. Hailman's private classes, he couldn't wait to plunge into each new day. What would he learn new about the world today? It wasn't long before Louis realized that learning was the magic key to the miracles of the universe, and he couldn't get enough.

"You are a very promising student, Louis," his teacher said on the day of Louis's first report card. "I know your mother will be pleased with all these marks of *excellent.* Make sure you always continue your neat working habits as well. My compliments to your parents. They've started you off properly."

The teacher was right about Louis's parents. They were indeed proud of their son's progress. Frederika Brandeis had also been a good student during her Prague childhood. She and Louis's father had tried to stimulate in all their children a thirst for knowledge and a love of learning.

In later life Louis often recalled the long winter evenings spent at home among the family, which sometimes included Papa's brother, Samuel, and Mamma's brother, Lewis, and their wives.

After dinner they would all move into the cozy parlor where a fireplace was lit. Settling down in their wingbacked chairs, the men would light cigars. Mamma would supervise the clearing of the table, then walk across the entrance hall and close the sliding parlor doors. This was a signal to Fanny, already seated on her three-legged piano stool, to begin a Mozart sonata on the grand piano, which had made the journey from Europe with the family in 1849.

Afterward one of the uncles would say, "Read to us, Louis," which he would do. That started them off on discussions and conversations lasting until late at night.

Louis was walking home from the Louisville Male High School one afternoon when a thought long in his mind became a decision. He was a freshman now and fifteen years old. On his daily walks from Ninth and Chestnut Streets, where the school was situated, to their big new home on Broadway, there was ample time for lengthy thoughts.

Louis was tall for his age, still thin, but he always stood up straight and acted determined, as if he knew exactly where he was going. Now that he had planned his important step, he was impatient to talk about it to his favorite uncle, Lewis Dembitz. When Uncle Lewis came to the Brandeis home later that week, Louis asked to speak to him alone.

"Uncle Lewis, I want to tell you of a decision I have made."

Uncle Lewis, comfortably seated and lighting his cigar, looked at his nephew, so serious and yet so sure, standing before him. "Of course, Louis. What is it?"

"First, I wish your permission to change my middle name from David to Dembitz in honor of you."

A bit startled, Uncle Lewis blinked at Louis. "Why, that's very flattering, I'm sure, but have you told your mother about this?"

"No, sir, not before receiving your permission."

"You are handling this very correctly, I see. Yes, Louis, I believe I would be very proud if you were to carry the name of Dembitz with that of your father. I have high hopes of your bringing great honor to both names, son."

"Thank you, Uncle Lewis. I am sure Mamma will agree to let me use her maiden name. Papa has only the highest regard for you, as we all have, and he will give me his approval, I am certain. As for bringing honor to the families, I wish to discuss another decision with you."

"Sure, Louis. What can I do for you?"

Sitting opposite his uncle now, Louis looked him straight in the eye, as he always did when addressing serious thoughts to another person.

"This concerns my future, uncle, but it also involves the feelings of Papa, and I will need your advice on how to best present the idea to him in a pleasing way."

Uncle Lewis sat very still, not wishing to interrupt his nephew, for he sensed that what Louis had to say would be of lasting importance to them both.

"I will begin this by telling you how very much I admire you, Uncle Lewis. I am sure you are the smartest man I know. I don't mean only those many languages you speak and read, or your knowledge of mathematics, or the many facts you can always bring to any subject you talk about. What I suppose I mean is the way you handle life in general.

"I want to be like you in as many ways as I can. First, I would like to begin by studying law, as you did."

Now it was Uncle Lewis's turn to look his nephew straight in the eye. What he had to say made Louis very happy.

"Louis, this time I must thank you for those extremely nice remarks. But I will admit something to you which I have felt for a long while. I think you and I are very much alike, not only because we both like reading a lot and love mathematics. But I suspect in you lies a great concern for the welfare of other human beings and an interest in all things that make up the world of people. You will have a great deal to give to life, Louis. It probably won't matter what field you enter, for there are so many ways to serve people. Perhaps you could be a very good doctor like your uncle Samuel Brandeis, or a successful merchant like your Papa. With your love of figures and charts, business is losing a good prospect, I suspect.

"I must tell you, however, that I feel the law is the best instrument for change—change for the better, that is. Civilization has always depended on its laws for progress, and there is still a long road ahead yet for progress.

"Yes, Louis, I am very certain you will make a fine lawyer, perhaps one history may even remember. I will be delighted to speak with your father about it. But you may find him more lenient than you think. It will be a disappointment not to have you follow him in the business which he has built up with all his efforts. But nothing matters more to your Papa than his children's happiness, Louis. He has realized for some time that your interests are not in commercial things, but in the world of ideas. I know your father will never stand in your way, if you choose the law; he will support you if you convince him that is the field for you."

Uncle Lewis was right about Papa. Adolph Brandeis's first concern was that his children lead a life of service to others. He and his wife had planted in them a deep sense of duty. The methods they would use in putting it into practice would be their own.

The following year, when he was sixteen, Louis was awarded a gold medal for "preeminence in all his studies." At the award ceremony Louis saw his beaming parents in the audience. Sitting on the stage, he did not show his emotions, but inside he almost burst with pleasure at the honor he had given his parents. He knew this was but the first milestone.

T W O

One midnight Louis's mother awoke to sounds of the violin drifting out of her son's room. She rose, carefully put on her robe, and tiptoed out of her bedroom so her husband wouldn't be disturbed. Louis stood in the middle of his room, peering at the notes on the music stand, while playing his violin in the candlelight.

"Louis, what in the world are you doing in the middle of the night?"

Louis gently put down his bowing arm. "But Ma, I'm practicing, of course."

"Do you know what time it is, son?"

"Sure, Ma. It must be around half-past six."

Frederika was torn between smiling at her son's mistake and feeling proud at his persistence in doing his work.

"Darling, it's actually around twelve o'clock midnight."

"Oh, Ma, how did that happen? I guess I misread my watch. It was so dark in here. . . . Hope I didn't wake anybody else."

"No, dear. I'm sure everybody is fast asleep. But you should be, too. Go back to bed, Louis. You need the extra hours. Good night, Louis."

Frederika walked back to her room, but she couldn't fall sleep again. Many things were disquieting her these days. Big things which were better kept from the children.

It was 1872. The war had been over several years, but the long shadows it had cast over the whole country still lingered. Now these shadows had approached them directly.

A big depression had hit many businesses in the land, a kind of panic which sometimes occurs after a war. The Brandeis firm which had done so well in recent years was tottering. It would be better to close it now before they lost any more money, her husband had said, and that's what he planned to do soon.

That summer Adolph Brandeis had a big surprise in store for his family. "Children, we'll be traveling to Europe next month. It's going to be a most exciting trip for us all."

Louis looked around at the stunned faces of Alfred, Fanny, and Amy. The silence lasted for only a moment. Then they sprinted toward their father, clamoring in joy for his attention.

"Oh, Papa, what a surprise! Where are we going? How long are we going to stay there? What about school?"

"Wait just a second. One question at a time, folks." Papa was pleased at the effect his announcement had had.

"We'll be sailing for England in August aboard

1. *Frederika (left), mother, and Adolph Brandeis, (right), father, of Louis Dembitz Brandeis*

2. *Louis D. Brandeis as he appeared at the age of 15 (left) and at 21 (right)*

the S. S. *Adriatic.* From there we'll go to Germany, Austria, Italy, and Switzerland. It may take us over a year to see all the places I have in mind. I am sure it will be an experience for us to remember."

Louis began a diary in which he recorded all the events of that important journey, which lasted far longer than his father had anticipated when they left Louisville that May of 1872.

It was a trip that served as a source of many memories which he stored up and drew from the rest of his life. The family traveled together until October, touring Europe and enjoying the many attractions along the way. Louis stayed in Vienna that winter, pursuing all the interests he loved: attending lectures at the university, visiting the theater, and listening to concerts. How he loved those months of study and pleasure.

When spring came Louis joined his family in Italy. Again they traveled together, savoring all the art treasures that country holds. They were on their way to the city of Milan when sister Fanny complained of feeling horribly ill. Feverish, she could barely stand up until they got to the hotel and found a doctor who diagnosed her ailment as typhoid fever.

The Brandeises remained together in Italy until Fanny recuperated, then journeyed to Switzerland so she could regain her strength in the natural beauty of the mountain country. With a worried eye, each family member watched her progress. Somehow she seemed so fragile now. . . .

The time came when Louis and his parents had to think of continuing his schooling. He had enjoyed his year of traveling and private lessons, but it did not take the place of regular school. If he wanted to pursue the study of law, he had to start some formal courses now.

Louis wanted to attend the Annen Realschule in Dresden, Germany, which had been recommended to him as a fine preparatory school. He had heard that it was necessary to pass the stiff entrance examination before a student could enter there. His family was still attending to sister Fanny in Switzerland and could not go with him, as they had wished to do. But a friend who knew the principal of the school had promised to accompany Louis.

Louis arrived in Dresden by train, feeling lonesome and deserted. His friend had not been able to meet him. For the first time in his seventeen years Louis stood on his own two feet. How would he make out in this foreign country, without family or friends to urge him on or encourage him when he needed a pat on the back? For several hours Louis walked around the grounds of the school, trying to give himself a push to go in for an interview with the principal or *Rektor*, as he was called in German.

Finally he overcame his timidity, walked in, and had himself announced to the principal.

The principal received him in his book-lined study, seated in a dark leather chair behind a high, imposing desk. Louis explained to him that he wished to be admitted to the school and showed his papers and report cards, which he had brought from Louisville, including the gold medal which he had been awarded for outstanding scholarship and conduct.

"Herr Brandeis," the principal observed, "I am very impressed by all the recommendations you bring me."

Louis breathed a little easier. He was standing in front of the principal, erect and tall, eyes fastened on the man.

"In your case I am even willing to forget the examination which is part of our entrance requirement. I am sure you are well qualified to be a student at our school. However, there is still one technicality which I cannot overlook which may keep you from entering this institution. We will need your birth certificate and proof that you have been vaccinated."

A slight smile played around Louis's curled-up lips as he countered the principal in his best German, with the soft Louisville accent.

"Herr Rektor, I should think that my being here is proof enough of my birth. As for my vaccination, perhaps, sir, you could check my arm and find there the scar to give you evidence you need."

The principal looked up sharply. What kind of a young man was this, who with a few words sought to abolish rules which had been traditional in his school? Had he been trying to be rude? But Louis looked at him calmly and pleasantly. There was something about this boy which appealed to the principal's sense of logic. For an American he was highly cultured and knowledgeable. But that must be due to his European-born parents. Or was it the boy's personality? He liked that young Brandeis. It might even be good for the school to have him here.

He arose from his chair and held out his right hand to Louis. "Herr Brandeis, it will be my pleasure to welcome you as a student at the Annen Realschule. Good luck."

Louis stayed at the Dresden school for two years and again, as at home, proved what an excellent student he was. Again he received awards for his conduct and the high caliber of his work. He felt that he was fortunate to have come to Germany, for he was fluent in his parents' language and able to absorb so much of the learning available here. Once in a while he felt a small twinge of homesickness for Louisville and the carefree days of his childhood. Much as he enjoyed the privileges of studying abroad there were times when the discipline of this Teutonic environment strangled him. It seemed ridiculous to keep such a tight rein on the students when with a little more freedom they might have a chance to show their own spunk.

One night Louis was returning to the school after an evening out. He reached into his pocket for his key—and found nothing there. He must have forgotten it when he left the dormitory that afternoon. He stationed himself under the window of his room and let out a low whistle, hoping that this would awaken his roommate who could let him in. No answer. Louis tried again, this time louder.

Suddenly he felt a strong hand on his shoulder. Louis whirled around and stared into the face of a blue-coated policeman.

"Mein Herr, please come with me."

Louis sputtered, "Why, what's wrong, Herr Polizist?"

"Don't you know that it is ungentlemanly and against the rules for people to whistle after hours, the way you just did?"

The closed face of the policeman would admit no excuse, Louis sensed. He did not bother explaining why he had whistled. It would have been useless anyway. The policeman was determined to puff himself up with his own importance. Louis had no choice but to listen to his strong reprimand. At least he was spared an official arrest.

Kentucky seemed very far off that night. Louis was very angry, more angry than he ever remembered being before. He knew that his offense had been a very minor one. In fact, nowhere but in this country of blind obedience would it have been an offense at all for a schoolboy to whistle at night. He missed the freedom of the land he had left behind and became more determined that he would do whatever he could to insure the permanence of such personal freedom once he got back home.

What had Uncle Lewis told him that day in the house on Broadway—"In law there is the greatest chance for progress." Well, he, Louis Dembitz Brandeis, would do his part.

Suddenly he knew it was time to go home to America. What he had been given was precious. He couldn't wait to put his learning into practice.

THREE

On a mild May evening in 1875 their ship approached New York harbor. Louis and his father, in need of exercise after dinner, walked around the deck. The steamer, its sails unfurled for steadiness, glided into home port. Many passengers lined her rails. Louis and his father joined the crowds watching the ship's progress.

"We've all been a little homesick for this moment, I think," Papa said.

Louis watched the pink clouds through which the last rays of the sun broke. On shore a myriad of windows reflected the golden glow. "I guess we didn't know just how much we missed home," he nodded.

In his diary he had recorded many impressions of the three years they had spent abroad. The book was filled with observations of the cities and the people he had seen. One observation he had not written down. He had only sensed it until now, but a change had come over his family's feeling and thinking. Louis, leaning against the ship's railing watching land draw near, suddenly knew what the change was.

"We are really coming home," Papa said. "All the years in Louisville we were still immigrants, feeling our way in the new country, becoming accustomed to a new life, yet remaining different. When we left on our visit to Europe, Mamma and I may have secretly thought of it as going home. Perhaps we expected it to be what we remembered—or wanted to remember. But now . . . well, I think we saw for ourselves why we left Europe in the 1840s. The reasons are still there. Only we have changed. I am very happy to be coming home, son."

Yes, Louis decided, the trip had done them all good. The Brandeis family had returned as Americans, fully convinced that their future lay with and in the New World.

The sun had gone down behind the pink clouds. Soon the shore lights twinkled their welcome. It was too late to let passengers debark this day. Tomorrow they would leave the ship and head for Massachusetts. Louis's mind was full of future plans. He believed more than ever he wanted to study law.

He needed an eastern school, one free from the narrow ideas which still hung over some schools of the South years after the war. He wanted to be a lawyer for all the people, not only the privileged. Louis was certain that Harvard was the right school. He had to persuade the Harvard authorities now that he was the right student for them. While his parents and the girls visited with relatives, he would travel to Cambridge and see about admission to the law school in the fall. His lips turned up in a smile as he remembered the scene in Dresden two years ago. What would it be like this time?

That fall Louis sat in a classroom of the Harvard Law School for the first time. The bright September sun outside the open window invited strolling on the leafy campus, but Louis was fully concentrated on the lecturer at the head of the room. He carefully absorbed every word of the speaker. A debate would follow this lecture and he wanted to be prepared. Louis felt he had a double responsibility to do well—a debt both to his school and to his family. He was only eighteen years old, younger than most of his fellow students. The Harvard Law School had admitted him without a college degree such as the other young men around him possessed. He had to do his best to prove to the school trustees that their opinion of him was justified.

Louis ran his hands over his eyes and let his eyelids close for a moment's rest. All summer he had studied books on American law, so he would be ready for the entrance examination. Sometimes his eyes grew red-rimmed from reading too much.

He would write home later today. The folks would want to know how his first school day went. Already he missed them all. It had been hard on them, too, to see him go—and not only for sentimental reasons. When he left for Cambridge it was Alfred who had offered him the several hundred dollars necessary for his tuition and living expenses at the school. Papa hadn't had time to get on his business feet again so soon after their long trip. Alfred, however, had been back in Louisville for some months and was beginning to do well.

During the classroom debate Louis noticed that the young man at the desk nearest him was an enthusiastic participant who not only liked to offer his opinions but apparently also knew what he was talking about. Louis liked the way this fellow looked. He was pleased when the young man came over to shake hands with him after class dismissal.

"I'm Sam Warren, from Boston," he volunteered. "I know you're Brandeis—saw it written on your notebook. Where you from, Brandeis?"

"Louisville, Kentucky," smiled Louis.

"My goodness, a southerner among all these Yankees. Well, I hope you'll be happy up here, Brandeis. Anything I can do? Are you comfortable in your lodgings? How about dinner together tonight?"

Louis smiled at the eagerness of his new companion. "I am quite prepared to like it here. Thank you for your concern, Warren. Looks as if it will be an interesting year. What'd you think of our lecturer? Pretty clever fellow, I thought. . . ."

"Shall we walk around a bit before our next class starts? I hate to waste all this good weather being indoors."

They walked toward the door, already enjoying each other's company.

"Do you want to know the name of a good riding stable nearby?" Warren asked him. "Being a Kentuckian, you must like riding."

"You read my thoughts. After so much studying all summer, I am getting quite stiff. Riding would help to get the knots out of my body.

"Incidentally, Sam, what is your opinion of this way of learning the law? You know, many trained lawyers feel that book learning is quite useless— the only way to get an idea of practical law, they say, is to apprentice in a law office for a year. Do you agree to that?"

Suddenly he stopped walking, "Oh, before we get too far . . . I *would* like to have dinner with you tonight."

It did not take Louis long to discover he loved Harvard—the courses, the library, the social life. He wrote long, detailed letters home about "his wonderful years" at the law school which kept his family and friends informed about his activities and his progress. His reputation as a splendid student soon spread through the school. It was to Louis that other students turned with their problems; it was Louis the professors enjoyed seeing after classes and during social hours too. His grades were outstanding. They set a record for years to come. Mamma and his father were so proud of him.

Then one day Louis received a profoundly disturbing letter from home.

"I wish I could do more for you, Louis. Nothing is harder for me to tell you. There is no more money for your education. I can barely pay my debts."

Poor Papa, how much pain this letter must have cost him, Louis thought. After all those years of providing so well for his family; those lovely vacations in the East, the three years in Europe with all the exciting opportunities for learning. Well, Papa had done what he could. And so had Alfred in his way, with his advances and loans. It was time for Louis to look after himself, and this was the time to start.

There was no doubt in Louis's mind that he must continue his studies somehow. He discussed applying for a scholarship with his advisor at Harvard. But his teacher was against accepting a scholarship.

"Why don't you tutor?" he asked Louis. "My son can be your first pupil. With your reputation you will soon have others."

Louis agreed and soon found himself a much sought-after teacher with many students to fill his spare time. He enjoyed teaching. He also thrived on his success in earning his tuition and living expenses. It was an exciting feeling, this knowledge that everything he spent he had earned alone.

I guess Father's business misfortunes have taught me something, he reflected. *One must have the means to live well, but never be so dependent on it that one's worldly goods become too important.*

A note from one of his professors reached him one day. "We are having Mr. Ralph Waldo Emerson with us next Tuesday evening. If it interests you to meet him, please come."

When he arrived home from an evening well spent in the company of interesting and important people, Louis always carefully noted his impressions down in the notebook he kept or in letters to his family. His early tidy school habits helped him in this record-keeping. If in his reading an idea struck him as worthwhile, he would write it down in his diary and refer to it when he needed to.

He relished this time of reading, meeting stimulating people, and learning from both. Sometimes he felt more tired than he liked, and he was troubled that his eyes hurt him so often. Urged by letters from home, Louis went to a gymnasium near the school and started doing exercises to get himself more fit.

During summer vacation in Louisville, Louis, sitting on the back porch with a book on his lap, suddenly felt his eyes getting dim and the letters on the page swim away out of focus.

Mamma had been sitting near him, writing letters on a little white table. She looked up when Louis shuddered with a sigh.

"Why, darling, what's the matter? You look so white. Louis, what's wrong?" She rose in her chair, because Louis had slumped forward, his hands to his eyes.

"Ma, it feels as if there is no more power behind my eyes. As if a light has been turned off. I . . . can't . . . see, Ma."

Frederika Brandeis did not panic. She was frightened, but she wouldn't let Louis know this. All winter, during Louis's first year at Harvard, she had worried about her son's health. She knew him well—how he would go on with his work even though he should have rested more. She was sure he had done far more than he should have. She also knew the determination with which her son attacked his every goal. Even when it was more than he ought to handle.

"Louis, dear, you have probably been out here in the sun too long. Come upstairs and stretch out on your bed for a while. I'll pull down the shades and you'll rest your eyes a bit. The dark, cool room will help, dear."

Louis knew his parents had worried about him. Their letters always warned him of abusing his health. He was not a complainer, but now he wished he could air his feelings a little. What had happened to his eyes? Would they get better? What in heaven's name would he do if they didn't?

Louis had a sick feeling inside as he followed Mamma upstairs. He didn't dare think of what might happen to his studies, to his future as a lawyer. Better control himself, he thought, take one step at a time. What was it his Grandpa Dembitz used to say when there was trouble in the family? *Kommt Zeit, kommt Rat* ... the solution will come in time. Ah, yes, his grandfather was a wise man. Louis stretched out on the bed and let the cool compresses which Mamma made for him soothe his burning eyes.

"Eyestrain," the specialist pronounced, "severe case of eyestrain, young man. The best thing I can advise is to stop reading altogether for several months."

Louis's father and mother had decided to make the two-hour train trip to Cincinnati with their son to visit the prominent eye doctor who had just examined Louis. Now they sat in the consultation room. Louis still sat in the examination chair, while the doctor finished putting drops into Louis's eyes to relax the muscles. Adolph Brandeis and his wife were seated in straight wooden chairs against the wall. In the semidarkness of the room they almost blended into the wall paneling. Louis sensed their disappointment at the doctor's verdict.

"I am sorry to give you bad news." The doctor straightened out his instruments and tightened the caps on several small bottles of eye drops.

"It is a big blow to you as a law student. I can't just tell you to stop pursuing your law studies, young man. But . . . well, to be honest, you must consider your health first, and I am afraid your eyes are not up to so much work."

Louis, his throat tight, avoided looking in the direction of his parents' chairs. "Doctor, isn't there a chance my eyes will get stronger if I rest them for a while, as you prescribed?"

"Mr. Brandeis, I must be honest with you. I don't know. It depends on how much you will rest your eyes. Much of the treatment is up to you."

It was a gloomy trip back to Louisville. The Ohio River, threading in and out of a summery Kentucky landscape, played hide-and-seek with the train. Louis was absorbed in thought. He didn't want to make his parents more miserable than they already were. But he was shaken by the doctor's words. What would he do if he couldn't go on studying law? The train wheels click-clacked through his brain, *But I must, but I must, but I must. . .*

They sat in silence, trying to find a way out. Louis's father sat in his upholstered plush seat staring at the countryside moving past them.

"Why do we have to listen to only one man?" he suddenly said. He turned toward Louis and his mother, sitting opposite him in the compartment, equally silent.

"There is more than one eye specialist in this country, you know. I am sure this man gave us proper advice, and for your sake, Louis, I would try it. But let's find someone else to examine your eyes —hear another opinion." Papa blew a big ring from his cigar, hoping to give himself and the others courage.

"You're right, Father. I'll take it slow for the rest of the vacation, then we'll see what happens."

To himself Louis thought, *Somehow I'll think of a solution, just like Grandpa's German saying. There is a solution to every problem—this one is a little harder than most. But it will come out all right . . . it will . . . it must. I can't let my dreams get away from me that easily. What would happen to the plans I made in Germany or the hopes Uncle Lewis has for me? Nothing will happen to them; I won't let anything be changed. The only change will be in the way I handle my situation.*

Louis had already begun to think like the great man he was destined to be. He looked at a problem from above and all around, not only from inside it. He could therefore see the whole of it. And because he was able to see a situation from all sides, he would find the correct remedy for it.

Louis followed his heart and returned to Harvard at the end of the summer. He also followed his father's advice and saw another eye specialist in New York that fall.

On his arrival at Cambridge, Louis called on his friend Samuel D. Warren at his lodgings.

"Sam, I'm going to need an enormous amount of help this semester, and I've come to you first."

"You? Help from me . . . or anybody? It seems unlikely. You, of all people, needing help. . . . But tell me what this is all about."

"I saw Dr. Knapp in New York this week—about my eyes. He is now the third doctor who has examined me. Actually, he confirmed what the other two have already said, that the cause of my trouble is a muscular weakness and that I should not use my eyes so much. But he said something the other two didn't. He said, 'Don't use your eyes, use your head,' and that gave me an idea."

Sam looked at his friend expectantly.

"How would it suit you to read me the assignments we must cover for our classes? Since we are in class together, it is material you should learn, too. Perhaps I could ask one or two of the other fellows to help out on this, so you wouldn't have the whole burden alone."

Sam held out his hand and Louis shook it.

"Louis, you know you can ask me for anything. Of course, I will read to you. Delighted to. When do we start?"

FOUR

A hurried meeting of the trustees of Harvard Law School was called on commencement morning of 1877.

"Gentlemen, a unique problem has arisen," the dean addressed them. "As you know, our school rules prescribe that a student must be at least twenty-one years old to be eligible for graduation. We have in today's graduating class a young man, Louis Brandeis, who is only twenty years old. Ordinarily we would not permit a suspension of the rules, but this is not an ordinary case. Gentlemen, Mr. Brandeis has in his two years with us achieved the highest grades that this school has ever bestowed. By rights he should be valedictorian of his class. I have called you here together to permit him to graduate.

"Clearly, Mr. Brandeis is a most unusually bright student. I am hoping you will agree with me and waive the rules, allowing him to graduate with his class this afternoon."

The trustees did permit Louis to graduate with his fellow students. The high grades he had earned during his second year of law school had proved the success of his idea. He had managed to turn a disability into a bonus. During the year just past, while his fellow students read his assignments to him, Louis trained his mind to retain all he learned. His memory became unusually keen. He stored away all information like material in a filing cabinet and when the proper moment came, pulled it out again and put it to use.

Louis was delighted with the personal victory he had won over the doctors' verdict. Yet he felt he needed to learn much more. So he returned to Cambridge for a third year of study, now on a graduate level. In this year, like in the previous two, he tutored and supervised examinations to support himself.

One day at the end of his year of graduate work, he handed his brother a check for the full amount of the loan Alfred had given him less than three years before, when Louis had started out for Cambridge and Harvard Law School.

Alfred, holding the check in his hand, looked at his younger brother with affection and pride. "You know, Louis," he said, "this is an important occasion for me, too. My best investment has paid off —in every possible way. We are awfully proud of your last three years. You've come up to every single expectation. Even in the financial department you've done well."

Louis raised an eyebrow at Alfred and smilingly inquired of his brother, "Why, Alfred, do you believe that you and Papa have a monopoly on the earning powers of this family?"

"The new firm of A. Brandeis and Son is doing well, thank goodness. In fact, we could now afford to hire a competent lawyer to represent us. Anyone you care to recommend, Louis?"

Louis looked away. He knew what Alfred was leading up to and he disliked the answer he would have to give him. It was the solution to a question with which he had wrestled for almost a whole year in Cambridge.

"Alfred, you are the first in the family to know about this: I have accepted a position in the law office of James Taussig in Saint Louis."

If Alfred was disappointed, he did not show it in his excitement over the news. "Oh boy"—he grabbed his brother's hand—"your first job. This is a big announcement. Congratulations! Shall we tell the folks right away?"

Louis hesitated slightly. "I hope I made the right decision," he said softly. "You see, I know how much all of you had hoped I would settle back here in Louisville after graduation. I would have liked to please Mamma and Father, and you, too, Alfred. After all, we have been separated from each other for three years now. But there is something else on my mind. I have no doubt that I could do well practicing law in Louisville. I would be wondering ever after, however, if my achievements were my own or due to my riding my family's coattails. This is no comfort if I achieve nothing. But if I accomplish something, it will be on my own, and that will give me much satisfaction. I need to prove myself on my own terms, Alfred. Do you understand what I am trying to say?"

"I'm afraid I understand you only too well, Louis. Yes, we had hoped you would come back here for good, it's true. Our parents have waited for the day when you would. It will hurt them a little—this decision of yours. But soon the hurt will give way to pride, for again you have chosen the harder way. It's so like you not to settle for the things that come easy."

Louis blushed. "I am lucky to have landed in such an understanding family. I am stepping on its toes, it seems, with every major decision I make, yet all of you back me up. You needn't make me out a hero, Alfred, just because I want to see how far I can go it alone."

"Your reasons are good ones, Louis, and all the more honorable because you could have done very well right here," he winked at Louis, "with family connections. When are you leaving us?"

"Taussig wants me there in September." Suddenly lean, tousled-haired Louis was the expectant boy again. "Gosh, can you imagine my name going up on that office door—Louis Dembitz Brandeis, Esq. At last, Alfred, at last I've gotten there. I know I'm not the type to show it, but you know, old pal, I'm pretty excited and fluttery inside. I certainly hope all will work out well in Saint Louis."

"You know it will, boy. But you're not going to be alone. Sister Fanny will more than make up for your leaving home. She'll do all she can to make things comfortable for you there."

In November 1878 Louis Dembitz Brandeis was admitted to the bar in the state of Missouri.

In his later years Brandeis often wondered what happened during his stay in the city of Saint Louis to make his time there so unhappy. But when the letter came from Boston, the letter which was to change his life, Louis was ready for it.

"Dear Louis," wrote his friend Samuel D. Warren, "Boston, not Saint Louis, is the right place for you. All of your many friends here miss you. I am trying to remedy this situation by suggesting that you and I become law partners right here. What do you say?"

Louis, who was never impetuous, who always weighed the advantages against the disadvantages, could find very little in favor of his remaining in Saint Louis. His law cases were not very interesting, the social life was dull, the climate suited him badly. He longed for the cultural atmosphere he had so loved in Cambridge.

At the end of the same day Louis walked the downtown streets of Saint Louis to the telegraph office and sent off a wire to Boston:

SHALL WRITE FULLY TONIGHT. IT SEEMS A GOOD THING.

Louis stood at the open window, looking down on the brisk street traffic below. He breathed deeply of the fresh air coming into 60 Devonshire Street. Oh, it was good to be back in Boston. Was it really only a year since he had repaid his brother's loan and set out for Saint Louis? How fast those months had gone by. Here he was in his own law office! Of course, it was only a one-room office on the third floor of a downtown Boston office building, but the firm of Warren and Brandeis was off to a good start. It even had its own messenger boy, at the extravagant weekly salary of three dollars.

Louis stretched and bid the street scene farewell before he turned and sat down at his desk. It was late afternoon. He had a long day behind him and several hours of work still ahead.

"Hi, how's Boston's most eligible young lawyer?"

Sam Warren had walked into the office, his happy bounciness announced by the creaking floorboards.

"A little tired today, thank you. Getting up at five-thirty doesn't mix with late evening hours, but life is too exciting to sleep it away. So we do the best we can."

"Have you fallen asleep at the justice's yet?"

Sam was joking, of course. He knew of Louis's deep interest in his work as law clerk to Chief Justice Gray of the Massachusetts Supreme Court.

"Oh, I hope that'll never happen. I'm learning too much in my mornings at his office—you know, he's really a very kind man, despite his reputation."

"Louis, it must be you. He likes you and thinks highly of you. To everyone else he appears severe and gruff."

Sam shuffled the mail on his desk into one heap before jumping up again. "I've got to go over to the law library once more. How about a turn on the river before it gets dark, Louis?"

"I'd like that, Sam. Especially after a day of figures and facts. Shall we meet back here at seven?"

"Fine. I'll run on then and see you later. Don't forget to bring your good suit along. Remember our invitation to the Delands tonight."

And he was out of the door.

Louis was grateful for Sam Warren's friendship. They spent much of their spare time together. There was always so much to do in Boston. Louis liked best the social life after business hours. This was the "life in the mind" of Uncle Lewis's world he had always admired so much. Now he had it for his own.

No one seemed to mind that he was Jewish or that his parents had been immigrants in this elite circle of Boston society to which his friend and partner had introduced him. Here it mattered that he was a success at parties, at literary gatherings, concerts, and charity affairs.

Law cases were coming in now as he and Sam slowly established themselves in the professional world of Boston. But Louis had not forgotten his dream of someday teaching law to others. He wondered whether he should pursue this dream.

In front of him lay the letter he had just received from President Eliot of Harvard Law School, inviting him to teach a course there the following year —at a salary of one thousand dollars for two lectures a week.

This was an offer too good to refuse. Louis opened his desk drawer to pull out an envelope, addressed it to his parents in Louisville, and slid into it the letter from President Eliot. As he sealed the envelope, he thought of the morning he had received the gold medal at Louisville Male High School and his parents' happy faces in the auditorium audience. He would have like to see their faces again and be present to watch their joy upon reading this letter.

He couldn't see their faces, but their written words reached him very quickly, and that was a way of sharing their pride in him, too.

"My dearest child, how happy you make me feel! My heart is a prayer of thanksgiving," wrote Mamma.

Papa wrote separately. "It is the greatest honor that can be given to a young man of your age."

The following week still another letter reached him—this one from Uncle Lewis.

"Last Friday night your mother came to our house near ten o'clock with President Eliot's letter of appointment in her hand, addressed to you as 'Louis Dembitz Brandeis.' It's the first time I felt glad at your changing your middle name from David to Dembitz. Your grandfather, if he could know of it, would be but too happy in knowing that one bearing his name has achieved an academic office, for none had a greater veneration than he for anything connected with the university."

Louis taught his course at Harvard Law School so well that afterward the faculty offered him a more permanent position: an assistant professorship.

Once again he had to choose between practicing law and teaching it. Now that he had had his taste of teaching, Louis did not like giving up his connections with the teaching profession or with life at Harvard University. He had become very active in alumni affairs and in the publication of the *Harvard Law Review.*

"I believe Harvard ought to be for students from all over the country," he wrote; "not only those living in the eastern states should have a chance of attending." And he began corresponding with alumni scattered throughout the United States who might be helpful in persuading bright young men to come to Harvard.

Always practical, Louis kept his eyes open for any opportunity to aid the school and help it grow. Passing a park bench in Boston Commons one day, he recognized a former classmate whom he had tutored during law school days. He waved.

"Oh, Mr. Brandeis, how are you? I am so pleased to see you again. It's been such a long time since school."

"Thank you, Mr. Weld. It has been a while, yes. But, wait a minute . . . you've been in the news lately, haven't you? Yes, of course, the inheritance."

Louis was referring to the sum of several million dollars which his former pupil had just inherited from his grandfather.

"To tell the truth, Mr. Brandeis, it's becoming rather a nuisance. Everybody in the state seems after me these days with a hard luck story."

Hands behind his back, Louis nodded gravely as his ex-classmate chatted on.

"Walk with me a little, Weld. My office is on Devonshire. I am on my way there now. I think I might have an interesting proposition for you which is worth discussing, if you have a few minutes."

As they sauntered across the vast city park Louis unfolded his plan.

"Perhaps you'll consider this as another hard luck story. In a way it is, yet I would prefer to think of it as an investment in search of an investor. Do you remember all the enthusiastic publicity which Oliver Wendell Holmes received for his lectures at our alma mater this past winter?"

"I had heard they were great, but I didn't attend them."

"I did hear one—it was superb. Made me wish I were back in school, with Holmes as the teacher. It's a little late for us, friend, but several of the alumni decided to raise some money so others after us can have that chance. The idea is that with enough funds available, we could get Holmes to accept a full-time professorship. How would you like to be the one to endow this project?"

Weld's eyes lit up. "It would be a great chance to repay my debt to Harvard for everything I learned there."

"Not only that. You'd also have an opportunity to make the school even greater. We've already raised the money for a new building and a large library fund. A chair for Holmes would really give the law school enormous prestige, don't you agree?"

"It sounds fine, Mr. Brandeis."

"Well, if this idea appeals to you, Weld, why don't you drop by Professor Thayer's office and talk it over with him. The two of you could probably work out a suitable plan."

Louis's efforts were appreciated by the staff and trustees of the law school. To show their gratitude to their former undergraduate, they admitted Louis to Phi Beta Kappa in 1890, and the following year he received an honorary Master of Arts degree.

I wish I could help the University of Louisville, too, especially its law school, Louis often thought. *I am still linked to the city of my birth in so many ways. I am discovering more and more that the strength of this country lies in its many local heritages and traditions. These should be encouraged to continue. The University of Louisville could become a fine school. It must express the people whom it serves and must express the community at its best. Someday I want to draw up a plan to help it along.*

Louis continued with his law practice instead of remaining on as a Harvard professor. He felt he needed more experience in trial cases, that courtroom procedures were a challenge of which he hadn't had enough. The odd pieces of information which Louis continually collected he quite often turned to his good advantage in court.

Once he represented a lady who was being sued by her landlord for damaging personal property while renting a house from him. Louis was trying to prove the landlord exorbitant in his claims.

In court as Louis questioned his witness in the chair, he casually glanced down at the list of damaged articles in his hand. "I notice that you list some damaged pillows here, sir. Would you be able to give us some details? How much did they weigh, for instance? With what were they stuffed, and how much did you originally pay for them?"

The landlord was slightly surprised by Louis's line of questioning, but he answered and named a price.

Louis turned to the jury. "Gentlemen, you have heard the amount just mentioned by the witness. I beg you to remember that our witness mentioned the pillows in question to contain fifty percent horsehair. Today's stock market quotation on the price of horsehair lists it at forty-one cents a pound. You will agree with me that the purchase price given us by the witness is about ten times the amount it ought to have been. If the price of the pillows is an indication of what we may expect to hear regarding other items on the list I hold, I would say the gentleman is making a substantial profit on his claim.

"Witness dismissed. Thank you."

The jury, impressed by Louis's apparent knowledge of his facts and the way he used them, voted in his client's favor.

After the trial the lady asked him how he happened to know so much about horsehair.

"Simple case of experience." Louis's eyes twinkled as he gathered his papers into his briefcase. "Several years ago my mother bought me a very good horsehair mattress. I studied the bill at the time and remembered the contents of the mattress and its price. I've been watching the price of horsehair on the stock exchange every day since. Never know when a little bit of knowledge will have its day in court."

FIVE

"Sam, I miss you at the office," Louis said to his friend at lunch one February day in 1890. "Your name is still on the door, but your cheerful presence is lacking."

Sam Warren picked up his napkin and spread it carefully over his lap.

"Yes, I miss those days of our early beginnings, too, Louis. If Dad hadn't died, Warren and Brandeis would still be complete. But I really had no choice but to dissolve our partnership. There was too much family business to attend to. An outsider couldn't cope with it. But it seems to me that you are far too busy now to miss a partner, Louis. You've been doing well. There's no lawyer who isn't aware of the name of Louis Brandeis."

"Life has been good to me, it's true, Sam. I couldn't wish for more. I've had some interesting law cases. I've made some wonderful friends here in Boston—and some enemies too."

Sam's face clouded. "I shouldn't tell you this, Louis, but last week I overheard a man at the Union Club say, 'Brandeis thinks he is the judge; he picks only the clients whom he believes to be right.' "

Louis put down his coffee cup and shrugged his shoulders. "I am not practicing law to make friends. I feel it more important to do the right thing than to be popular. After all, I don't want to turn my back on my ideals. Several times lately I have excused myself from cases which offended my sense of justice. I feel it is more honest to say so than to defend an unjust cause."

"Of course, Louis. But do watch your step. It will help your career to be on the right side of your fellow lawyers."

"You mean well, Sam, I know. I am sometimes compelled to go my own way, but I appreciate your advice. Today I met you purposely to ask it."

Sam sat very still. His eyes rested expectantly on Louis.

Louis toyed with a teaspoon, then carefully replaced it on the table. "After twelve years of working at a successful law practice, I am becoming restless. I am tempted to try something bigger. I must admit that for some time I have thought about public service, yet I haven't been sure just how to go about it."

"But you've been doing that, Louis, all along."

"You mean those civic reforms clubs I belong to? Well, yes, they serve their purpose in a local sort of a way. What I have in mind has no direction yet, except that it should serve the common good."

"You have the potential for leadership."

"I do have the desire to be of service. There is

a pressure from within—a deep sense of obligation. Perhaps it isn't the big businessman who needs my help, but the little fellow, the one who works for him."

"Have you thought of entering politics?"

"Yes, but that wouldn't be the right solution for me. Besides, can you picture a Jew in Boston politics, Sam?"

"You know that wouldn't apply to you, Louis. You are well known and liked by many influential people in this city."

Louis put his hand on the arm of his friend. "It is precisely that which would put me into bondage. I would have to consider those well-meaning people in every move I make, and I am sure I would step on someone's toes every time I plan a single campaign. No, friend, politics isn't for me."

Sam smoothed out a wrinkle in the white tablecloth. Then he straightened up to study the face of his ex-partner.

"You want to champion the underdog. Why, Louis?"

"I am not sure. My Jewish background must have something to do with it. Jews have been underdogs in so much of their history that they identify with the underprivileged and feel the urge to help when they are in a position to do something about it. Perhaps my own family history proves it. My parents weren't willing to be underdogs—that's why they left Europe. And when they came to this country they became abolitionists because they couldn't tolerate the idea of keeping other humans enslaved.

3. *Louis D. Brandeis in a portrait at the time President Wilson nominated him to the U.S. Supreme Court (1916)*

"From my family I have received this feeling of obligation to attempt to better things, to work at changes to improve the lot of less fortunate ones. It is the duty of the privileged to lead the way."

"Hey, look at that." Sam's eyes were riveted on the headlines of the afternoon newspaper held by the man at the next table:

STRIKERS FIGHTING PINKERTONS IN BATTLE OVER WAGES

"Waiter, please bring us a paper," Louis requested.

Together they read. "Homestead, Pennsylvania," the article was datelined. "The plant of the Carnegie-Illinois Steel Company was the scene of pitched battles yesterday as strikebreakers hired by the company were fighting striking workers who had refused a wage cut by the steel firm. Many were injured as the workers, barricaded on land, fought it out with men of the Pinkerton Detective Agency who were located on barges in the Monongahela River. Violence lasted all day."

Louis shook his head unhappily as they read on about the first major labor conflict in American industry.

"Now labor and management must resort to open warfare because they cannot agree on wages," he said to Sam. "How can anything be settled by violence like this?"

In his imagination Louis could see the workers lashing out with their fists and clubs in the damp dawn mists of the river. He was growing excited.

"This is no way to secure one's rights—nor for bosses to treat their workers. It defies all democratic principles."

"Well, Louis, here's your answer. You've got yourself a brand new career and your first problem—"

"How to bring the worker and his boss to agree to proper working conditions and a decent salary," Louis finished. "I must change a lot of my thinking, Sam. You know, life is advancing so rapidly in our day, the old rules no longer apply. With industry growing so fast, our laws are not equipped to keep pace with it. From now on the big companies will play the important role in our country's progress. It is especially important that the individual be protected, otherwise he will get swallowed up in the race to power."

"Remember when Justice Gray said of you, 'I consider Brandeis the most ingenious and original lawyer I ever met'? You were only twenty-four when he wrote that, Louis. I have a feeling you will follow him to the U.S. Supreme Court some day."

Louis put his head back and laughed heartily at his friend's words. He had blushed to the roots of his unruly hair at the compliment Sam paid him, but the corners of his deep-set eyes were crinkled in amusement.

"Before I go that far, Sam, I've got a lot to learn. First, I better cancel that course in business law I was to teach at M.I.T. This strike changes the whole picture of American labor. I better bone up on my homework."

"Mr. Brandeis, telegram for you."

It was the landlady knocking on the brown oak door of his room. Louis had heard the ring at the front doorbell a few minutes earlier and sensed that the early morning call held bad news for him.

He had known for several weeks that his sister Fanny was seriously ill. As he opened the telegram from Louisville, he trembled a little.

FANNY GONE. COME HOME.
ALFRED

Louis sat down in the big armchair nearest his bed, telegram in hand. Now that it had happened, now that all their fears of recent months had come true, he was numb. He thought of their stay in Switzerland years ago when the whole family had worried so much about Fanny's recovery from typhoid fever.

Fragile, witty Fanny, his favorite sister. She had always been such good company. Even when she was ailing she had brightened life for others. Louis thought of the musical evenings of his childhood. How talented Fanny had been. Her brothers and sister couldn't touch her skill and knowledge of playing the piano.

If it hadn't been for Fanny and Charlie, I would have perished of homesickness in Saint Louis, Louis thought. Fanny, as a young housewife in Saint Louis, had given so much warmth to her brother's stay there.

The cold winds of March blew outside as Louis packed his suitcase for his sad journey to Kentucky. It was starting to snow as he got into the horse-drawn cab which was to take him to the railroad station. Looking up at the gray, heavy-hanging skies, Louis felt cold and lonely. Suddenly he longed for a family of his own to cushion him against the blows of life.

In the week following Fanny's funeral the Brandeis house was constantly filled with people paying condolence calls. Louis felt especially alone. As he looked around, it seemed that even in their grief everyone had a mate or a partner with whom to share it. His parents had each other, Alfred had a wife, his sister Amy had a husband.

He walked out of the house one afternoon and headed for the home of his uncle Dr. Sam Brandeis. It would be good to talk to Uncle Sam awhile, Louis thought, and to Aunt Lottie too, with whom he connected many happy childhood memories.

As he stepped into the hall of his uncle's house, Louis heard voices in the library. His ear was attracted to an unfamiliar but melodious feminine voice laughing in response to a joke by Uncle Sam.

Louis followed the sound into the room and found his uncle sipping coffee with a tall, brown-haired young woman whose simple white dress contrasted handsomely with her dark good looks.

"Louis, my boy, how wonderful to see you. Come in and join us."

Louis half advanced into the library, his eyes riveted on the girl in white. She calmly deposited her cup on the coffee table in front of her and smilingly met Louis's gaze.

Uncle Sam stood up and walked toward Louis.

Putting his hand on his nephew's arm, he pulled him into the room.

"Don't you remember your second cousin Alice —Alice Goldmark from New York? You knew each other as children when the families vacationed together in Newport."

"I remember you, Louis," the warm, musical voice said. "The busy little boy who never sat still long enough for me to talk to him. You were always engaged in sports or in fishing, and if I saw you reading, I didn't dare disturb you—you were so absorbed in your books."

Uncle Sam laughed out loud. "I better warn you, Alice. He's still like that."

Alice motioned with her hand toward a spot on the sofa next to her. "Sit down, Louis, I'm happy to see you again so many years later. But I am truly sorry we're meeting at a time so sad for you."

"When did you come?"

"We arrived in Louisville just two days ago—too late for the funeral services, but of course we had no idea about poor Fanny."

"We?"

"Yes, my brother Henry and I. He's touring some of the western states on an engineering survey and I came along to sight-see."

"Oh." Louis suddenly felt relieved.

"I think Louis is happy to know you're not married, Alice. Isn't that right?"

Louis blushed. What's the matter with me? he wondered. Me, a grown man in my thirties, a successful lawyer pleading causes in Boston courts, acting like a schoolboy.

Her pleasant laugh put him at ease. "Uncle Sam's

a tease. Don't let him get you. He's been calling me an old maid ever since I arrived, and I play right along with him, eh, uncle?"

The doorbell rang then and Uncle Sam went out to see who was at the door. When he came back, he excused himself. "I've got to see a patient who's running a high fever. I won't be long. Do you two think you'll get along without me for a little while?" He winked at them both.

Alice laughed her melodious laugh again. "We'll be fine, uncle. We'll discuss all the years between Newport and now. You just take your time."

She turned to Louis. "Would you like to walk a bit, Louis? I believe we're great walkers on both sides of the family, as far as I can tell from observing my Kentucky relatives."

Louis enjoyed the company of this beautiful girl who could look him in the eyes with the straightforward manner of an old friend. He felt as if he had known her for years. Apparently she was equally at ease with him. She matched his walking step and took his arm when they approached the street corner, casually keeping up a steady conversation.

Louis asked about Dr. Joseph Goldmark, Alice's father. Dr. Goldmark had led a highly exciting life —starting with his student days as a member of the Academic Legion, which in 1848 had fought on the barricades of Vienna.

"It must be a great satisfaction to have fought for the freedom of others and see your cause become victorious."

"But, Louis, you should know that feeling of

satisfaction yourself." Her face was close to his, her dark eyes sparkling. "Your battles in court probably benefit an even greater number of people in the long run than Daddy's bayonet-carrying friends ever managed."

Louis stood still. The girl's head came up to his shoulder as she stood facing him, straight and slim. The strong winter winds clutched at them both, but Louis barely felt a breeze.

"Why, what do you know about my court cases?"

"Enough to know that you are fighting some fairly important battles yourself. The outcome of some of your law cases may make life a good bit easier for many people who would otherwise have been oppressed by their employers and their working conditions."

"How do you know about these things, Alice?"

"I read the papers, I talk to people, I see for myself. And if I find that a second cousin of mine, a Mr. Louis Brandeis, concerns himself with problems which interest me too, I make it my business to be informed."

"You surprise me, Alice."

"Why, Louis?"

"It is unusual for a girl as pretty as you to be involved with problems of society. Dances and beaux and dresses, yes . . . but conditions of the working class, well . . . you are different, Alice. Delightfully so."

Alice's color heightened, just enough to let Louis know his remark had pleased her.

"These are exciting times, Louis. You, of all people, are aware of that. Everyone, man or woman, has a duty to look out for the welfare of other people. Even if this weren't the time in history for social awareness, our religious tradition has always taught us that—it is part of us, whether we always realize it or not."

Louis suddenly knew that he wanted to see more of this earnest girl, who did not let her femininity get in the way of her ideals. As he walked her back to Dr. Sam Brandeis's house, he told her he would stay only a few days longer.

"Before I leave Louisville, may I call on you again, Alice?"

"Oh yes," she replied and added, as if to temper her eagerness, "I would like that very much, Louis."

When Louis left his uncle's home that afternoon his heart felt lighter than it had in many a day.

They met again in August of that year. The Goldmark and Brandeis families vacationed in the Adirondack Mountains, and Louis spent a few days with them.

These were wonderful days, for now Louis was sure he had found the one person with whom he wanted to spend the rest of his life and discovered that Alice felt the same about him.

"Your Boston friends will lose their star attraction—the eligible bachelor," Alice laughed.

"Miss Goldmark"—he gave her a courtly bow— "that's a title I would have gladly given up years ago had I known you were in the world with me."

And hand in hand they started off for an afternoon's sail on the lake.

The wedding took place in the Goldmarks' New York apartment on a Sunday afternoon in March 1891.

Only the closest family members were seated in the large Park Avenue living room as Louis and Alice stood before the small dais erected between the double windows and repeated their vows to one another.

"I now pronounce you man and wife."

All during the ceremony Louis had not taken his eyes from his bride. Now Alice turned to him, smiling, and Louis marveled at the overwhelming happiness he felt.

How right everything had worked for him since that afternoon twelve months ago when he walked to his Uncle Sam's house. The loneliness he had experienced that day would never again hit him as hard. With Alice by his side to share his successes, and his disappointments too, life could only be good from now on. After the struggles of the day were done, she would be there, welcoming him home.

"Congratulations, old man." His brother, Alfred, clapped him on the back and kissed the bride. "Very thoughtful of you to get married on my birthday, Louis. You're a lucky fellow . . . got yourself a good wife."

"Thank you and happy birthday again, Alfred. You're right about my being fortunate. But I just can't understand it—all these many years I have stood on my own feet, worked alone, and managed to get ahead, but now everything is changed. This young lady has worked herself into my life, and I

cannot do without her advice and approval any-
more."

The bridal couple turned to face the room. The
afternoon sun streamed in through the windows
behind them and in its glow stood the tall, smiling
young man with the dark, pretty woman clinging
to his arm. An air of contented happiness cir-
culated through the crowd as the families congratulated the newly married pair and then each
other. It was a perfect match, they all agreed. Louis
and Alice were made for each other. They would
bring out the best in one another—these two hand-
some, intelligent people whose joy their families
shared today.

"A toast to the bride and groom."

Papa raised his wineglass and everyone in the
room applauded consent.

"Dear children," he began, "all of us wish you
lifelong happiness together. May you have only joy
and success and the love of one another. May you,
and those who follow after you, know the full blessings of this wonderful country, and may you always
continue to repay those blessings so that others in
turn may benefit by your good fortune."

Louis and Alice started married life in a house on Boston's Beacon Hill. When Louis bought their red brick, wrought-iron-trimmed home on Mount Vernon Street he was well aware of the historical background of the area and of its antique beauty. He also knew that most of their new neighbors were people of wealth and accomplishment. As the son of former immigrants, he was conscious of that continuous line of American aristocracy carried on by the people living up and down the street. He liked the feeling. It gave him a reassuring touch of permanence and of belonging.

By the time he was in his middle thirties, Louis Brandeis was already a wealthy man. But to him money and honors were of no importance—only a means with which to carry out the projects he believed significant. He and Alice preferred to live simply and spend no more then they actually needed.

The many interesting guests who stepped over the round cobblestones of the driveway into 114

Mount Vernon Street may have looked for elegant interiors and a lavish table. They found instead that an invitation to the Brandeis home meant genial hosts and a room filled with good conversation. Though the modesty of the furnishings may have surprised some, the high level of discussion stimulated all who came.

These early days of his marriage were happy indeed. When his daughter Susan was born in February 1893, followed three years later by the arrival of Elizabeth, Louis's dream of family life was fulfilled. Now he had children of his own to whom he might one day pass on the results of his efforts to better the working and living conditions of his fellow man.

It was in 1902 that Louis received an office visit from his acquaintance William H. McElwain, a wealthy Massachusetts shoe manufacturer.

"I need your help, Louis. My plant in New Hampshire is on strike, and nothing I can think of seems to settle the problem."

That night one window remained brightly lit in the house on Beacon Hill. Long after his dinner company had gone home, Louis sat at his desk, intensely studying the figures on the graphs and charts before him. The flame of the gas jet flickered in the room. Suddenly a shadow fell on the paper. Alice silently placed a glass of milk on the corner of his working table.

"Oh, darling, I didn't want you to wait up for me," said Louis apologetically.

"I felt guilty falling asleep, knowing you were still working."

"I'm sorry, dear. I am finishing up the preliminary facts for my trip to New Hampshire later this week. You know I try never to be unprepared."

"It's an important case, isn't it?" Alice, attired in a pretty pink peignoir, settled down on the divan opposite Louis's desk.

"I feel that it will be. It interests me for two reasons. Of course, Bill McElwain is my friend and I want to help him. But he is also an intelligent employer who wants to do the right thing, and he will listen to my recommendations. So I am hoping to get McElwain and the head of his union to sit down together and talk over their problems. This will be a new way to settle a strike. Owners of businesses must understand the troubles that beset their employees and give some consideration to them."

"Why are these people striking?"

"McElwain's factory is working on a piecework system, and the work is only seasonal. The pay is good while there's work, but when they've run out of orders, the factory is shut down and all the workers are without income. To protest against such a system, all the union people have walked out."

"How do you hope to have both parties agree to a solution, Louis?"

"I have looked over the figures McElwain brought me. You know I base all my decisions on a study of figures—to me there's no truer picture of a situation—so I want the owner and the union to work out a schedule which gives the employees yearly work. It can be done."

"It would help if they cooperated with one another."

"Ah, Alice, perhaps you should have been a lawyer, too. You hit the heart of the problem. Nothing would remain unresolved if there were true cooperation between two parties. In time, I am sure, the labor unions will become powerful enough to be listened to. We haven't reached that stage yet. We still have to impress the employer to make him recognize the worker's right to join a labor union. So many owners fire personnel when they find a union is involved. And if they do have union workers at their plant, some employers do not always deal fairly with them or their representatives."

Louis's success in settling the New Hampshire strike brought him acclaim in the legal profession and a national reputation as a labor mediator. After the local reforms, other cases followed in which Louis took the side of the public against utility companies and other large concerns that Louis felt were not fair or responsible to the people they supposedly served. Because Louis did not accept any fees in these public service cases, he soon earned the nickname of "People's Advocate."

The road which Louis Brandeis wanted to travel, and was to travel for the rest of his long career, was now clearly laid out for him.

But it was a rocky road, one which cost him the friendships of many of his former clients and friends, who could not understand Louis's interest in the welfare of the general public when he had formerly been doing so well representing the big companies which they headed.

"It's a good thing you are on my side," he said wearily to Alice after a long heated court battle against the Boston Gas Company had been victoriously concluded. "As I walked home from the office tonight, I remembered the warning Professor Shaler, my old counselor at law school, once gave me: 'You're too sensitive for active public life.' Well, it's not only costing me money in lost client's fees, but I must swallow all the accusations which come my way and never show how much they hurt. Tonight the newspapers are printing an opinion that I surely have an ulterior motive in my public service work. Now they have me seeking the mayoralty of Boston in return for my troubles."

"But you won the case, Louis. It's a great victory for the citizens of Boston. In your last big campaign all the users of the tramways and the subways benefited when the fares were lowered. This time the consumers of gas in the area will be paying less."

"And the rights of the people are preserved. That's the most important part, Alice. The bills we got through legislature will keep the public service companies in check, we hope. These great companies must serve the public, not become power-wielding instruments for their stockholders."

"Oh, Louis, I *am* proud of you. You've done so much in recent months, worked so hard, and sustained so many annoyances. Don't you think you could—"

"Alice, dear, I know what you are going to propose—a vacation."

"The girls and I had hoped to see a little more of you again. Susan could use some help with her woodworking projects. She is planning a full-size dollhouse and needs your steady hand."

"In August we will take our regular vacation together again, as always. And I might be able to help Susan over the weekends. But there is so very much to do. Plans must be made, speeches composed and delivered, committees formed, and letters written. One person cannot manage it alone, but the work, if properly organized and handled, will go on. I have some excellent people to help. Good government does not just happen. It is the duty of every single citizen to be informed and to act according to his information. So we must get the facts to the public. How can we pass on to our children a heritage which is tarnished and corrupt?"

Alice came and stood behind him, her hands on his shoulders. People were saying that her husband was beginning to resemble Abraham Lincoln. Now, as she saw his profile silhouetted against the declining daylight beyond the open window, she could almost believe it—the thin, pointed face, the deeply recessed eyes, the weary shoulders. Her heart was moved by the force which propelled Louis to pursue his goal relentlessly through all opposition.

"You know how very much I agree with everything you do, dear. I'll always be here for you."

Louis darted her a grateful glance. "I need and appreciate that support, darling."

Alice walked around until she stood facing him.

"There are times when I cannot understand why the big, fundamental problems you are fighting—poverty, unemployment, long working hours—are so difficult to solve. It would occur to almost any child that these things are evil," she said.

"Nothing changes without a struggle. No single forward step is taken without lengthy legal battles. Then bills are pushed through legislatures, and then finally conditions are bettered."

"Well, tomorrow you will go at it again, knowing you are doing right and giving your time, energy, and money to your work."

Louis stood up and stood tall. "It keeps me on my toes matching my wits against the high-priced legal counsel hired by my opponents."

"Is there anyone as clever as Mr. Brandeis?" Alice's perky laughter cheered him and, as always, restored him to his purpose.

"I am a fortunate man. It's a good thing not all my opponents have wives as wonderful as mine. I have a suspicion that's the secret of my success."

Fall had seldom been lovelier than it was this year of 1907 in the city of Boston, Louis decided, stepping through the fallen leaves of October-hued Mount Vernon Street. Other men might prefer their chauffeur-driven automobiles, but he cherished his homeward strolls from the office. He loved to walk off troubling thoughts. The nearer he came to his home, the more refreshed was his mind.

As he turned into his driveway he saw that Alice was awaiting him in the doorway, a pleased expression on her face. Holding the front door closed behind her, she imparted the news to him.

"Louis, dear, we have unexpected visitors. Josephine is here, and she brought her boss, Florence Kelley. I suspect they came on business, traveling here from New York. I asked them to have dinner with us first and told them you would talk to them later."

Louis left his briefcase and hat on the hall table, then walked into the parlor. He embraced his sister-in-law, Josephine Goldmark, and shook hands with Mrs. Kelley, whom he knew as the head of the National Consumer's League. He was especially fond of his wife's sister because she so actively carried out the Goldmark ideals in her work in behalf of women and child labor laws. He sensed that it was this cause which brought the two ladies to see him.

He was right. Mrs. Kelley waited until dinner had relaxed them all, then asked if she might speak of the purpose of their visit.

"Mr. Brandeis, I know what a taxing year this has been for you; perhaps it is an imposition to ask you to take on something altogether new. Yet we are looking for a man of the highest legal stature, and we feel that in you we have found him. Josephine has encouraged me to think that this case might interest you sufficiently to undertake it, so I will let her explain it to you."

Josephine spoke hurriedly. "Louis, we have just found out that an Oregon employer is testing the ten-hour labor law for women in the Supreme Court. It is absolutely vital that this law be upheld, for many other states now also have women's labor laws which would be threatened if Oregon lost this suit. We need you to assist the attorney general of Oregon in pleading this case."

Louis leaned forward in his chair, hands folded, fingertips touching.

"Tell me something of its background," he demanded.

Mrs. Kelley took up the story. "The owner of a laundry in Portland, Curt Muller, forced one of his women employees to work longer than the ten hours a day permitted for women employed in laundries and factories. The employee, a Mrs. Gotcher, took him to court, and Mr. Muller was convicted and fined.

"But Mr. Muller was not satisfied with this verdict, especially after he talked to other laundry owners and found out that the U.S. Supreme Court had recently ruled against another ten-hour work limit—one affecting bakery workers in New York State. Mr. Muller and his friends wanted to test the strength of the Oregon law, so they are taking it to the Supreme Court."

Louis got up and measuredly paced the width of his study, his hands clasped behind his back. "I would need an invitation from the attorney general," he began thoughtfully, "so I could actively–"

Josephine jumped up and rushed toward him. "Oh, Louis, you'll take it?"

"With so much charming persuasion, I have no choice but to accept. However, I will have to rely upon you heavily," he addressed Josephine. "You must do the investigating for me, all the detail work with which to prepare for such a case. This time we have a chance to get at the heart of this women's labor law and we must not fail. Are you willing, Josephine?"

On a late snowy afternoon in January 1908, Louis boarded the Washington-Boston Express for his return home. Gingerly, he climbed the icy train steps carefully clutching the green briefcase against him.

As the engine gathered speed in the darkening landscape, lights twinkled on everywhere in the frosty world outside. Inside, Louis struggled to calm himself from the hundreds of candles dancing in his heart.

This day he had stood before the highest tribunal of the land and argued a case which he knew would have the widest influence in bettering working conditions for women from now on. He, the immigrant's son, had by his own wits and efforts tried to persuade the Supreme Court of the United States to enforce a law which forbade the exploitation of working women. In ever-widening circles this law would lead to other laws, and in time the life of the working class of America would earn the respect and envy of the whole world.

Would the court respond to his plea? The old men in their black robes appeared forbidding enough when they entered the judicial chamber. For a while Louis wondered how his thoughts could penetrate. These men looked dried and withered like parchment, unable to absorb new ideas.

But he had been so sure of his cause. When he stood up for his presentation, the butterflies in his stomach soon disappeared. His voice rang out loud and clear. Newspapers had written that his voice could hypnotize an audience. Well, he had tried this morning. If the verdict turned out unfavorable, he would try again and again.

Louis looked lovingly at the briefcase which he had placed on the seat opposite him. Josephine had done her job well. From her impressive research he had fashioned a document of a hundred pages—pages that almost cried out with human voices as Louis listed, in country after country and generation after generation, the details he needed to make his appeal. Artfully he had woven a tapestry of the reasons why women should not be forced to work more hours than those prescribed by the ten-hour labor law.

And then he had summed it up. "Women are not physically as strong as men and need more rest," he had argued. "Since they are also mothers of children, we must guard against impairing the health of future generations."

Louis's statement included only two pages of legal reasons for his stand in behalf of the labor law. The major part of his defense was based on social and moral reasons with which he sought to prove that overworking women was wrong.

As he sat down after his summation, Louis noticed the white-gloved hands of Josephine and Mrs. Kelley wave in greeting from the visitors' gallery.

"Tickets, may I see your tickets, sir?" The train

conductor slid open the compartment door. Louis handed the ticket to the agent, who punched and returned it. "Thank you. Hope you had a good day in Washington, sir." With a smile he disappeared into the corridor.

I guess it has been a good day, thought Louis as he settled back into his seat. *Can't wait to tell Alice all about it.*

Six weeks after his appearance before the Supreme Court, the case of Muller *v.* Oregon was decided in favor of Louis's client. Oregon kept its labor law. So did the other states whose social progress might have been arrested had the verdict returned been different.

In the summing up, the presiding justice mentioned specifically the voluminous work done by Mr. Louis D. Brandeis in his brief presented before the court.

Not only were the Supreme Court justices receptive to this new approach, but with this mention, the term "Brandeis brief" entered the language of law.

SEVEN

Susan and Elizabeth Brandeis chased each other down the stairs and bounded eagerly into the large, sunlit dining room. At the head of the rectangular table, napkin unfolded on his lap, their father was seated, waiting for them. The hall clock chimed seven as the girls began the most exciting part of their day. Unless their father was out of town, this hour with him was theirs alone. Breakfast over, Louis and his daughters spent an hour reading. Seated around the table they talked of many things interesting to them, but history, literature, and current events were of special importance. The girls treasured this time with their father. It gave them a share in his thoughts.

They were reading a book on Roman history one morning when Susan, then a teenager, casually interrupted to ask, "What is a trustbuster, Father?"

Louis looked up from the book, surprised. Was this his older daughter, who always displayed such good manners? He pondered Susan's face. Then he quietly closed the pages of the volume they had just studied.

"You read last night's newspaper, I see. Well, these days that's one of the nicer things they call me, and it's not really a bad thing to be."

"But what does it mean, Father?"

"A term the newspapers coined for a person who fights monopolies in business. As you know, in America our century is an era of bigness. Small groups of men control giant industrial empires which reach out into every branch of American life. Such a system which regulates the price of its products and has exclusive powers over it is called a—"

"Monopoly," finished the younger girl, Elizabeth, when he looked her way.

"Right. A monopoly or a trust."

"But why is that bad?"

"I believe business monopolies are evil because they deprive the small man of his chance to compete in trade. They also hurt the country financially. Monopolies can, if they wish, sell to customers they select, rather than to the general public. They can also keep the salaries of their workers low, knowing that no other similar jobs are available. Now, all these things are extremely harmful. They will cause great damage to our democratic system if men of responsibility do not check them."

"And that's why you're fighting the New Haven Railroad?"

Louis laughed. "No, Susan, it's not that simple. But I think I may find a way of explaining it to you."

He walked over to the china closet, opened the

door, and took out a small Meissen figure, a little shepherd boy, which he carefully deposited on the dining table before the eyes of his daughters.

"This piece of porcelain and I have something in common. Both of us have been to Dresden, Germany. The china was molded there, but I also received a lasting impression in that city. I went to school in Dresden, as you know. I was almost arrested there one night because I had the audacity to whistle on the street after dark. That encounter with German law I regarded as an infringement of my personal freedom. That same evening I determined that I would fight for freedom, whether mine or someone else's, so that in my country, at least, there would be no such infringement.

"I have since learned that infringement of one's personal freedom can take other forms. The right to compete for one's share in earning a proper living, for instance. The right not to have to work long, hard hours at little pay. Freedom is not a privilege of the well-to-do. It is a right belonging to everybody, or it should be. So I fight my battles as I see them—and hope that Americans of every layer of society will be better off as a result." Gingerly, he carried the blue-and-white china figure back to the cabinet and replaced it.

"All except Mr. J. P. Morgan, Sr.," added Susan.

"He is presently the most powerful man in America, but there are many others of immense fortunes who seek to improve their personal riches and influence with every business move they make."

"What is Mr. Morgan like?" persisted Susan.

"Does he really look like a devil?" Elizabeth wanted to know.

"If I were to say yes to that, Elizabeth, I would be no better than the people who write unpleasant things about me in the newspapers. It so happens that I have never met Mr. Morgan in person. All my cases in the courts have been against people who work for him. But I have seen pictures of him. He is a very tall man, always dressed in black, holding a cane with a golden knob. He has heavy black eyebrows and they curve in a peculiar way. That, and the fact that he never smiles, have given rise to talk that he has a certain satanic look. I suspect, however, that this might have originated with people not too happy with his business tactics."

Louis sat back, smiling slightly. With the fingers of his right hand he combed through his close-cropped tousled hair, now graying at the temples.

Susan was not to be put off. Like her father, she wanted to run things to their source and dig up the facts.

"But how did you get started doing this, Father? I mean the . . . you know, trust-busting."

"It is a story with several branches, Susan. One part of it began three years ago, in 1905, when a group of Boston businessmen came to me for help. 'Investigate conditions at the Equitable Life Assurance Society of New York for us,' they asked. 'We're policyholders and we think funds are being mismanaged.'

" 'I will undertake the investigation,' I told them then, 'but I want to act as a private citizen, not as

4. *Nathan Straus, Louis D. Brandeis, and Stephen S. Wise at the time of the founding of the American Jewish Congress in 1918*

5. *Louis D. Brandeis visiting his brother, Alfred, in Louisville in 1922*

your hired counsel. I will not accept a fee.' "

"How did you begin, Father?"

"With my favorite method: facts and figures. I studied figures during the day, and at night I took the books home with me. You girls were too young then to notice that I stayed up late every night until I learned that my suspicions had been right. Life insurance companies were very corrupt."

"You could tell that by their books?"

"Oh, yes. It showed. A few men in the corporation held all the power and drained the income of the company for their own private investments. They actually used the money of their policyholders in order to enrich themselves. The heaviest loser was the customer."

"Why?" Elizabeth asked. Both children's eyes were on his face.

"The low-income worker, the person who needed insurance the most, was in the majority of cases too poor to finish paying for his policy. Many times he had made payments in nickels and dimes at a real sacrifice. But when he could no longer finish paying, this money was not refunded to him. The insurance company was the richer for his loss."

"But that's cheating, isn't it?"

"Well, I thought so, and fortunately there were some people who agreed with me. They were the ones who backed me up when I proposed a solution."

Both girls looked up so expectantly that Louis had to smile again.

"I made many speeches and wrote magazine articles and in them I said: 'Let banks take over the function of the insurance companies. With their financial experience and their trained staffs they can offer a similar service to the insured at a much lower cost.' "

"Did it work?"

"First, I had to convince the general public. So I used the same weapons which were useful earlier in my tangles with the Boston transportation system and the gas company in the days when you girls were not yet born. I spoke wherever I found an audience, and I wrote for any publication willing to print my articles. There was no group too small for me to address. You ask Mother. She used to accompany me to most of these meetings. It did me good to know that at least one member of the audience was favorably disposed toward me." Louis grinned as he thought of his early crusading days.

"Finally, last year, after two years, the state of Massachusetts was won over. The legislature passed my bill to permit savings banks to handle life insurance under state supervision. It was another happy day in the Brandeis household. And do you know what the moral of the story is?" The tone of voice warned the girls their father was teasing, so they kept straight faces as he answered his own question. "If you can't solve it by law, you can solve it by mathematics."

The girls giggled appreciatively, flattered that their father had shared the story of his pet project with them.

It was a good thing Louis had decided early in his career not to let criticism and personal abuse by his opponents deter him. "Playing fair" was not a part of this game, and he learned to accept it without resorting to the same weapons in return.

When he became involved in fighting the management of the New Haven Railroad to keep them from acquiring locally owned Massachusetts railroad and trolley lines, Louis became the target of many poisonous insults. After some strongly anti-Semitic cartoons about him appeared in the newspapers, several friends came to call on him.

"There must be a way to stop this vicious propaganda campaign against you," one of his old friends said. "The public spirit and the generous devotion which your life so well exemplifies makes the lives of many of us seem despicably mean, sordid, and narrow."

To their amazement they found Louis cheerful and entirely optimistic. He thanked his friends for their concern.

"I learned long ago not to make denials against the vile charges brought against me. You see, if I denied any such attack, I would dignify it. And look how much time it would take away from my true task of fighting the methods of my opposition."

But as Louis continued to touch the nerve ends of important heads of business, they became more aggressive in their attacks upon him. "The chronic howler" they called him for uncovering ever more evidence that big business was not serving the public interest. The publicity worked in an unexpected way, too. Louis was now well known, not only in his own state, but nationwide. Magazines asked him for articles, and universities invited him to speak to their students on business matters.

"I have been asked to run for mayor of Boston," Louis wrote to Alfred, "but I thought it better to concentrate on fighting the railroad merger instead."

Too bad Papa could not live long enough to witness this latest link in Louis's chain of success. But when he passed away, in the midst of the campaign for savings bank life insurance, he knew that his youngest child was well on his way to fulfilling all the promises he had foreseen for Louis.

With his life so filled with the many tasks he had set for himself, Louis now had to forgo the trips home to Louisville which had been such a frequent and pleasant part of his younger days. And he missed the visits. Things were different with Papa gone, but family ties were as close as ever. The Brandeises in Kentucky were informed of every important undertaking Louis planned.

Step by step, they learned through letters to his brother of the progress Louis was making in his seven-year war against the New Haven Railroad and the management practices of J. P. Morgan. In 1914 the federal government stepped in and ordered the railroad to give up control of its smaller holdings. That ended the New England railroad monopoly and brought to a finish the longest, hardest-fought, and bitterest campaign Louis Brandeis had led.

His work took him often to Washington now. Louis knew to count on the hospitality of his friend Robert La Follette, senator from Wisconsin, whenever he was in town.

"You have a standing invitation to be with us whenever you can," Mrs. La Follette said to him after they had finished dinner on one of his visits. "You see, we all think most highly of you, but my husband feels closer to you than if he had known you for a lifetime. It is amazing how you two have become such fast friends in a short time."

Louis thanked his hostess. Then he drained his glass of port wine. "Though we have no common memories yet, we do share enemies," he agreed.

From the head of the table the senator said, "Some of the better rumors already have us hatching an evil plot against big business and blowing capitalism clear out of the country."

Louis wore a thin smile. He was tired and grateful when Mrs. La Follette broke up the after-dinner chatter so that the two men could discuss political matters in the senator's study. He was anxious to tell "Fighting Bob" the news he had heard that day. In this household he was certain of complete understanding.

Louis could hardly wait for the study door to close behind them and for Bob to settle in his desk chair before he burst out. "United Shoe has bought out Plant's business. It's the greatest flouting of justice I've come across. I tell you, it's something free men ought not to put up with." Agitatedly, he walked up and down as he told La Follette the details of the story.

The senator had already heard that Thomas G. Plant, inventor of some shoemaking machines, had tried to compete with the largest maker of such machinery, the United Shoe Machinery Company, which owned or had control over nearly all shoe factories in the eastern United States. Plant had attempted to sell his machinery to some eastern shoe manufacturers who were under contract to United.

"United Shoe was trying all sorts of devious ways to get Plant," Louis continued, still pacing. "For months they have been figuring out how to push him out of the business short of violating the anti-trust law. And do you know how they finally did it?" He wheeled and faced La Follette's desk.

Bob looked up, slowly shaking his head.

"By cutting off his credit. Not a bank in the East would lend him the necessary money for going on with his manufacturing. If anybody still needs proof that the money trust backs every industrial monopoly in the country, perhaps this shady trans-action will convince them."

"It's monstrous that such a thing can happen in this country," La Follette commiserated. "How does the story end?"

"The night before his bank loan came due—when he knew for certain he wouldn't get another—Plant went to the office of the attorney for United Shoe Machinery, who called in the officers of the company. All night they were at it, writing up papers and making Plant sign them, desperate as he was. Before morning came, the competitor of the United Shoe Machinery Company was through. I tell you, Bob, it's sickening to think of this in the spirit of what America once stood for. Where is freedom now, or the untarnished ideal of equal opportunity which brought our forebears to this land?"

Louis Brandeis was white with anger. Bob, who knew his friend as the cool, clever counsel whose composure no one had been known to ruffle, had not seen him like this before. The two men were much alike. Both believed the time had come for the lawlessness of the privileged to be curbed. La Follette did his part with fiery speeches in the Senate, and Brandeis with his work in the courts of the United States. The two had come to symbolize the spirit of progressive politics of their day.

Finally, Louis sat down in the chair opposite his friend. Together they began plans which they hoped would, in time, prevent Thomas Plant's story from being reenacted in America.

"Give me a list of people who you know have been pressured or been forced to sell out to the monopolies," La Follette suggested to Louis. "I won't name the true names, but I will use the material in some magazine articles I am writing. I hope to draw up another antitrust bill within a short time, so this information will come in handy then, too."

"I will be glad to. My files will provide ample material for your speeches," answered Louis. "I will also speak up in behalf of your bill in committee hearings before the Senate. Perhaps our combined efforts will gain more than blasts from our critics. At least, it is reassuring to know that in you

I have found a kindred soul, someone who believes as optimistically in the brighter future of the little man as I do."

"It takes constant work and vigilance and a thick skin, but it must—and will—be done."

"I am not sure that I believe punishment will do the trick." Louis stood up. He had pulled out his pocket watch, which showed the hour was late.

"Regulations, preventive measures might keep down big business to within its proper boundaries. This would be one method of avoiding future tragedies like Plant's. Federal commissions with set rules, that's what we need."

The federal government soon stepped into the United Shoe Machinery case and brought suit against the firm for violation of antitrust laws. The company was forced to disband.

Shortly afterward Louis appeared before a congressional hearing on yet another antitrust law.

"There used to be a certain glamour about big things," he stated. "Anything big, simply because it was big, seemed to be good and great."

Louis visualized the midnight session at which Thomas Plant had been forced to turn over his hopes to his creditors. In a sad voice he finished, "We are now coming to see that big things may be very bad and mean."

EIGHT

The New Hampshire woods were cool and remote
from courtroom battles the day in June when Louis
started a long introspective stroll through the pine
forest. The Brandeises, relaxing during their an-
nual vacation, were settling down to the peaceful
mood of their retreat. It was 1910, and for the first
time in several years Louis enjoyed his vacation
without giving a thought to the legal problems he
had left behind.

Just as he began his morning hike a note reached
him, brought in by messenger. He stuffed the letter
into his coat pocket and walked down the porch
steps of their little hotel. He was headed for the
woods.

The serene silence of the shaded paths made it
difficult to imagine another scene, one described
in the note now contained in his pocket. Not so far
away—in New York City—the summer sun shone
on hovels and tenement flats where the mood was
ugly and turmoil was about to erupt.

"Did you enjoy your walk, Louis?" Alice asked him when he had rejoined his ladies at lunch on the awning-covered terrace.

"It was delightful," he answered, but his face looked troubled. Alice sensed that his thoughts were far away. She waited until the meal was over and the girls had left them before she mentioned the problem on his mind.

"Bad news, dear?"

Louis sat up straighter. He had had that faraway look again, but now his eyes were caught in Alice's straight, questioning gaze and he was back in the present.

"The whole garment industry is going out on strike. Sixty thousand workers," he answered her, speaking each work distinctly. He reached into his pocket for the now-crumpled note he had carried all morning.

"From your friend Filene," she acknowledged after Louis had handed her the note. "He wants you to come to New York and see what you can do. Are you going?"

"No. I will have nothing to do with it."

Louis was so abrupt in his reply that his wife shot him another look. But she didn't speak. Louis would give her his reasons, in time.

"It will be difficult to settle. They are striking for a closed shop."

Alice knew of her husband's strong feelings against a system which forced the owner of a business to hire only union personnel. To him any form of coercion in business life was unfair, whether on the side of management or the worker. She sat in silence.

When Louis looked her way again she said, "A strike in the garment industry is really a civil war between Jewish workers and Jewish owners. What a marvelous thing it would be to have someone like you, Louis, arbitrate this—someone Jewish who could evaluate both sides of the problem in an impartial, fair way."

Louis put the note back into his pocket. He had a thoughtful expression on his face. "They haven't asked me to arbitrate, Alice. If they do, I am not at all certain I would accept."

"Louis, think about those people, poor souls, who are forced to work in the sweatshops. Those miserable hovels where women and children sit at sewing machines all day or work over a steam iron from morning till night for very little money."

She went on hastily, almost apologetically. "Of course, I know how much you've already done, expecially with your interest in women's labor laws and child labor laws. But think of the chance you would have of really helping these people!"

Alice leaned forward and tenderly covered Louis's hand with her own. There was a light in her eyes. Louis suddenly remembered the day on the wind-swept Louisville sidewalk when he had accompanied Alice on their first walk. Perhaps she was thinking of that day too, the day she had told him of her admiration for his work.

"Dear, what a God-given opportunity you'd have for service to your *own* people. Oh yes, I know you've always thought of yourself as an American first, doing things to help all Americans. But you're a Jew, too, and these are your people. This is an area that needs all the reforms for which you have worked over the years—what a boon it would be for these people who came to this country looking for the Promised Land."

"Your enthusiasm is just as inspiring as in the days when we first met, darling," said Louis. "I know the deplorable conditions under which workers in the garment trades must work, often because their fellow religionists use every means to exploit them. It isn't a simple situation to solve unless both sides are agreeable. I am not sure I could do any good."

The summons arrived a few days later in the form of a telegram. A committee representing both sides of the strike had been organized. This group was looking for an eminent person to mediate a settlement. Louis Brandeis, in their estimation, was the perfect choice as their arbitrator. . . .

Louis's train had just rolled into Grand Central Terminal in New York. A short, dark-haired young man rushed through the moving crowds and approached Louis as he descended the few steps from the Pullman car.

"Mr. Brandeis? I am your reception committee from the union. I was hoping I'd spot you right away. No trouble recognizing you. We're awfully glad you came down." The young man held out his hand in greeting. He had a gentle smile.

"Thank you. I hope your expectations will be

fulfilled and that I can do something for you." Louis looked around for his overnight bag. "Have you made any plans for my stay?"

"Yes, sir. You'll be staying at a nearby hotel. Since it is Saturday night and a warm evening, I was wondering whether you wouldn't like to come down to the East Side with me for a while. To sort of look things over. I borrowed a friend's car."

The young man was soft-spoken and serious. He spoke English well but had a strong accent. Louis guessed him to be from a Balkan country. After the stuffy club car on the train, the soft, warm night air in the open touring car felt refreshing. Louis was glad that his host had given him the chance for a closer look at the area of his latest efforts.

"Just call me Dave," the young man had said back at the railroad station when Louis had asked his name. Dave proved a good guide, providing information on all the sites along the way which might interest his passenger.

"This is the Essex Street Market," Dave announced after the drive downtown along Lexington Avenue had brought them to lower Broadway, then to Delancey Street. "Nothing you can't buy in this place. They have Jewish items from every part of the world." He pointed to the sidewalk stalls on either side of the street.

Further down along Broadway he showed Louis the building where *The Jewish Daily Forward* was written and printed, the newspaper which claimed to represent the Jewish worker.

"Tell me, Dave, what is your opinion of the strike?" Louis had to ask it. He was interested in this personable young man who was apparently a cultured, knowledgeable human being with an intense affection for the area he was showing to his guest.

"Mr. Brandeis, from now on I want you to look around very carefully. If you see the things I want you to see, you won't need my answer. Now when we turn the corner into Henry Street, I want to point out a very important building to you. You know about it I am sure. The Henry Street Settlement?"

"Yes, I am quite familiar with the work of Miss Lillian Wald, its head," Louis nodded. "A wonderful woman."

"That lady has done tremendous things for the immigrants in this area. She's an angel. But wait . . . now, Mr. Brandeis, now start looking around. Look at the houses."

Louis had a view of blocks and blocks of tenement buildings, all looking dingy and unkempt in the light of the streetlamps. Windows were open everywhere and people leaned out of them, gesturing to other people on the sidewalk. Women held diaper-clad babies on windowsills, showing off their size to neighbors. Little groups of men clustered in front of lighted stores, busily talking in Yiddish, newspapers under their arms.

"All the stores are closed on the Sabbath," Dave explained. "They've just reopened after sundown awhile ago. That's why you see so many people out on the street now. They're all talking about the strike. But Saturday night is usually their time for resting a bit. The only time they have in the week. They work terribly hard."

"And they work in these buildings, their homes, don't they?" Louis asked.

"Yes. You see, it's piecework they're doing. The work is given out by a manufacturer to a contractor, who farms it out to be done at home. Whole families are employed this way. They are not paid by the hour, but by the number of garments they produce. So their home becomes a factory where they try to turn out as many pieces as possible."

"Is this how you work too, Dave?"

"Yes, unhappily. When I arrived at Ellis Island from Lithuania, a former neighbor of my family was there at the pier. We didn't really know him too well in the village back home. Here he acted as if we had been best friends and offered me a job with his boss. I was a greenhorn, Mr. Brandeis. I didn't know the difference. I thought he was doing a *mitzvah*—a good deed—by looking out for me." Dave smiled a sad little smile. "You know who he was looking out for—himself. I should've known that."

"Why, Dave?"

"Well, the more people a subcontractor has working for him, the more prosperous he becomes. He can get more work from the manufacturer. He pays starvation wages to his workers, so they must turn out more merchandise if they want to live. But in the meantime, he gets more money."

"What about your own family, do they work like that, too?"

"Yes, my parents and my wife help me. I do the cutting in the front room of our flat. My father is a baster and a tailor—he works the sewing machine. My mother and my wife do the pressing. We always have a glowing iron going in our kitchen, summer and winter. Believe me, we sweat in there."

"But why, for heaven's sake, did you continue with this kind of work after you learned what an inferno it was? Surely a bright young man like you could have earned a living doing something else."

Dave studied the car's steering wheel carefully for a few minutes before he answered.

"Mr. Brandeis, I can see that this neighborhood is a new world to you. Perhaps you look down on us for being what we are, but I don't think so. I think you really want to help. That's why you came down from Boston tonight. Right? Well, please don't get angry at the way I'm talking to you, but I must get you to understand something. Have you ever been a penniless immigrant with fear at your heels?"

"No," said Louis in a low voice.

"I came over first," Dave continued, "because in my village there was no work for a young man if he was Jewish. I was going to pave the way for my parents, bring them over . . . support them. But a pogrom hit the village and they fled for their lives. They bundled up whatever they could carry in their arms and walked to the nearest big city. There relatives gave them money for steerage passage and helped them leave the country.

"I want you to know the background, Mr. Brandeis. It explains why we're glad to do any work we can get in the new country. We prefer to live together, even in a smelly neighborhood like this, because we know a fellow Jew isn't likely to touch a match to your roof. And if you work for a Jew, you know he'll give you time off for holidays and prayers, even if he docks your pay for it and makes you do overtime. But it's important for many of us who observe our religion faithfully."

Louis lowered his head pensively. He thought how right Alice had been about the opportunity for service. His people, yes. But how much he still needed to learn about them! Young Dave was unlocking a whole new world to him tonight. What a strange thing it was. Louis Brandeis, the Jew from Boston, was discovering his fellow Jews. What irony to have been the target of so many anti-Semitic attacks for years when he thought of himself primarily as an American. He knew practically nothing of Jews, their problems, and their fears.

Dave carefully piloted the car through cluttered, often narrow side streets to give his passenger a thorough, close look at the neighborhood.

Louis, still thinking over some of the things Dave had said, was troubled. "Dave," he finally said. "I see the reasons for the strike clearly now. Heaven knows, we must work out ways for better conditions than these. The home workshops should be abolished and more sanitary, better-lit surroundings provided. But frankly, I am puzzled. Why have people been willing to put up with this way of life for such a long time now? I see resignation on many faces and in the gestures of the people on the streets. I notice it in you, too. You are in America. There is every chance for betterment. Why does it take so long for our people to fight for their rights?"

"You are lucky, Mr. Brandeis. Forgive me for saying it. I've read about you, and I know you live in a world with big people, people with important names. You don't know the feeling of being Jewish in a world that hates Jews. Oh, perhaps you do." He raised his hand and shrugged his shoulder when Louis turned a surprised face at him. "I have read enough in the newspapers to know you get your share of attacks. But those are words plunged at you, not rifle butts. People like us, who've been driven from their homes—it takes them a long time to trust the world again. Sometimes it takes forever. Even this country isn't always paradise to an immigrant. The newcomer looks strange, talks strange, acts strange . . . and he knows it. So he sticks with the people who accept him and stays in a rut."

"You don't seem to me to be in a rut," Louis commented quietly.

"I am fortunate. I've discovered a means to better my lot—and that of others—in time. The union movement is our salvation. Only in numbers will we be able to convince our employers that we will stand up for our demands. This strike, now, is the beginning of our fight. We need the work or we starve. But the bosses, they need us just as much, for without workers there is no business."

"Your union must be glad to have you as a member. You are intelligent—and you are able to see the other side of the question."

"Well, if we can keep the hotheads down, our group will do all right."

"Let's hope that will work for both sides, Dave. You have managed to teach me something tonight. I think we had better go to the hotel now. I have an early morning meeting with the committee. If I am to do my best for a strike settlement, I'd better get some rest tonight."

Dave grinned. "Funny that I should teach you something, Mr. Brandeis. That wasn't the way I had expected the evening to end."

"We all learn from each other. But I'm grateful to you, Dave. Your tour of the Lower East Side tonight has been a revelation to me. I feel happy to have had you as a guide. Thank you, indeed."

In the weeks that followed, Louis had many occasions to think back upon the evening he spent discovering the way his fellow Jews lived and worked. Many times he wished that the committee members with whom he worked possessed the knowledge and sympathy displayed by his guide, Dave, on that tour. For these were very difficult weeks. Meeting after meeting was devoted to airing grievances which both sides held against each other. Often the workers turned against management, the owners against the employees. Sometimes both of them attacked Louis as chairman of the group of mediators.

It was a long, often discouraging summer. The garment industry was still idle. Several times when a successful settlement of the strike seemed near, a minor point would cause such objection by one side or the other that the whole peacemaking effort was threatened with collapse. In his diplomatic manner Louis would then address the committee: "Gentlemen, I have seldom seen such cooperation among opposing factions. I am pleased to be chairman of such an intelligent group." So with flattery and praise he would get them started on another round of talks.

When he was disheartened by lack of progress, Louis tried to think of the people he had seen milling about on the streets of lower New York that Saturday night in June. Weren't they entitled to a fair and just living after the suffering they had seen in their native lands? To those among them who, as immigrants, had been greeted in New York harbor by the Statue of Liberty with a promise, had that promise become reality?

"We must try harder, gentlemen. Much depends on what we accomplish here. So many await the outcome of a just settlement."

Finally on September 2, 1910, both sides signed the "Protocol of Peace."

A milestone had been reached in the world of labor relations. Sweatshops were to be abolished. There was to be no more work in the contractors' shops or at home. Not only could workers in the garment industry now count on more tolerable working places, but their working hours were also shortened and their wages increased. The employers could choose the workers they wanted to hire, as long as they selected union members. Best of all for both sides, permanent machinery for settling future strikes was set up, which took over when the management-union shop committee could not settle the dispute.

More time was to elapse before working reforms became as complete as labor leaders wished. But the "Protocol of Peace" was a start, a good start.

And Louis, traveling back to Boston, felt happy that he had said yes to that telegram from New York.

NINE

"What do *you* think of Zionism, Mr. Brandeis?"

It was not the first time Louis had been asked the question, which was dividing American Jews of his day. Reporters were always hoping for a Brandeis reply on controversial subjects to provide their newspapers with unusual copy.

Mr. Jacob de Haas was not another reporter, however. He was the editor of *The Jewish Advocate* of Boston, and he had come to South Yarmouth for a business meeting with Louis. The two men discussed how to raise funds for the Democratic party's election campaign that fall of 1912.

Now, their talk completed, Louis was seeing his visitor off at the railroad station near his vacation hideout. The question hung in midair.

A strong August sun invaded the shadows of the little waiting room, open on the side toward the train tracks. Louis removed his panama straw hat and dabbed a crisp white handkerchief over his forehead.

"The Zionists deserve much admiration. I have

watched with growing concern, along with every other Jew, the worsening situation for the Jewish people in Europe. The pogroms and persecutions of the East European countries should be a warning signal to all of us that the future of the Jews will not be on that continent."

"And do you think Palestine will be the solution?"

"I do."

"I am glad you feel that way, Mr. Brandeis. I remember that your uncle, Lewis Dembitz, was an early and ardent Zionist. He was a good Jew."

Louis turned halfway on the straight-backed wooden bench and eyed his guest.

"Yes, Uncle Lewis was a most unusual man. He had much to offer the world. I learned a great deal from him. My interest in Zionism did not stem from him, however. I must admit that most of my knowledge and sympathy for my people came from an experience I had in New York two years ago."

"The garment strike, yes," commented Mr. de Haas.

Surprised, Louis said, "You know about it?"

"I read many of your writings and observations during that time and I sensed that you were undergoing a transformation in your feelings toward the Jews."

"Transformation?"

"Yes, sir. The name of Louis Brandeis ranks high on the list of American leaders. Your accomplishments and achievements are almost legendary, though you are still a fairly young man. And yet, one element needed to be added. I am delighted that you have found it possible to be both a good American and a good Jew."

Louis looked puzzled. "Why do my views matter to you, Mr. de Haas?"

He was not sure whether to be irritated or flattered by this impertinent man with the British accent.

"I am looking for men who can bring the movement forward, who can be a help to the Jewish people in their desperate need. Only in a permanent home can they develop as a nation and be free from further persecution. To be honest, Mr. Brandeis, I have made this my mission ever since I had the privilege of working for Theodor Herzl."

"You? You worked for Herzl?" Louis asked, amazed at the revelations this man had to offer.

"Yes, during the years our great leader spent in London, I was his secretary there."

"And why are you here in this country now— permanently, I assume?"

"It was Mr. Herzl's belief that I could be of assistance to his vision of the Jewish homeland if I came over to America to spread his ideas."

Louis had read the writings of Theodor Herzl, the Austrian journalist who, seeing the plight of Europe's Jews, decided they would never be accepted as social equals even though they had attained political freedom in some countries. Herzl wrote a book, *The Jewish State*, in which he proposed that a gathering of all the world's Jews into one nation would solve many of their problems.

Louis stood up abruptly. "Mr. de Haas, you interest me. I would like to talk with you in more detail.

Could you spare me the time to chat over luncheon in my home and take a later train?"

The Boston-bound train left without de Haas that afternoon, while the two men walked back to the Brandeis vacation house. They spoke about the First Zionist Congress which had taken place in Basel, Switzerland, in 1897.

"The idea of a Jewish homeland is most worthwhile," Louis agreed with his companion. "I believe Jews have a gift for self-government. Certainly we should have a chance to try it."

"Does that mean, Mr. Brandeis, that you feel you could be active in the Zionist movement in America? You *are* a fighter."

"I am not really a fighter, Mr. de Haas, but I am a great believer in pursuing my goals with persistent effort."

"There is much opposition to Zionism in this country, sir. At this stage you would be fighting an unpopular cause."

Louis smiled his sad, sweet smile. "Sir, you must know that unpopular causes are my specialty."

"Your name would add great prestige to our efforts."

"The dreams and hopes which I have for all people certainly apply to the Jewish people as well. It would give me the greatest satisfaction if I could help to solve this most urgent dilemma of our people."

It's strange how the world reaches out to find you if the time is right and the cause important enough, thought Louis. Mr. de Haas's visit to South Yarmouth had stirred him. Long after his visitor had

departed on the early evening train to Boston,
Louis walked the dunes, alone with his thoughts.

He would become formally associated with the
American Zionist movement as soon as he returned from vacation. This would be only the first
step. Then he could begin to work more actively,
to do his part to make a vision come true.

A country for the Jews alone—where they could
rule themselves and support themselves—that *was*
a vision! It was almost unbelievable that he, too,
should be caught up in this creation. These many
years he had been removed from all things Jewish
and now he was full of enthusiasm about rebuilding the Jewish homeland.

He wouldn't find much support at home with his
newly found views. That was certain. Even Alice
might not share his opinions this time. Of course,
he knew Alfred would be sceptical about this in-
volvement in the Zionist movement.

Uncle Lewis, you would have approved, I know,
Louis thought. He recalled the evenings spent in
conversation with his favorite uncle so many years
ago. He bent down to pick up a handful of oyster
shells washed inland by the current. He raised his
arm and one by one threw them back out to sea.
Each shell raised a ripple before it sank.

*Perhaps this is the way your ideas found me after
all,* he mused, *leaving an impression I did not notice at the time. Rebuilding the Jewish homeland—
this would have appealed to you.*

A small state . . . not only a haven for the homeless, but an active, productive spot on earth. A
place where there could be true justice for Jews

and the brotherhood of man could become reality. *For the first time since Jerusalem fell, Jews will be holding up their heads in pride, knowing this land is theirs,* dreamed Louis. He was sure no Jew would settle for anything but the original homeland of Palestine, although other places had been discussed in official negotiations. All their prayers recalled it, all their songs sang of it—the Promised Land, the home of Abraham.

That's the way it should be, reflected Louis. A modern miracle in an ancient setting. A place where the old Hebrew language could be revived, where Jewish life could be lived the way it had begun, and where a heritage of three thousand years could be continued.

Louis stood facing Nantucket Sound, letting the vigorous evening breezes blow over him. He would help a miracle come true. It was a thought that filled him with unbelievable joy and lightened his steps as he turned toward home.

Less than two weeks later Louis traveled in the cabin of a New York-bound night boat. Mysterious sounds of river traffic reached his ears and were forgotten as he sat at a little table and studied once more the telegram he had received earlier that day at South Yarmouth.

MR. WILSON WISHES TO SEE YOU. PLEASE COME AT EARLIEST CONVENIENCE.

So now he was en route to meet the candidate he considered likely to win the presidential election in this critical year of 1912.

Woodrow Wilson, governor of New Jersey, had been nominated by the Democratic party two months before and was busily working on his campaign strategy. Many of the progressive ideas which Louis had championed in his years of public service were contained in the political platform of the Democratic nominee. Louis Brandeis supported Woodrow Wilson, for he knew his own life's work had a greater chance of being carried on if Wilson were elected.

Whenever Louis traveled aboard a ship, he remembered his trip home from his student days in Europe. What great, high dreams he had had as he stood at the ship's railing with Papa, wondering if his boyish ambitions would ever be realized.

Now, so many years later, he had learned that no matter how many ambitions had been fulfilled or how many plans had been brought to fruition, it would never be enough.

"There is always so much more to be done, so many problems still to be solved."

He walked over to the open porthole in his cabin. The night air smelled of seaweed. Bright, unclouded stars foretold a clear day.

Louis sensed he had reached another plateau in his career, which to him was interchangeable with his life. The son of immigrants was about to become advisor to a future president of the United States. It sounded pompous when one put it into words, and Louis disliked pomp. He felt serene, but also very pleased that his work had been worthwhile, his ideas deemed important enough to be put into practice by men of government.

He knew how fortunate he was to be able to devote his life to public service. For many years his law firm had run smoothly, without his presence but still carrying his name, providing generously for the living needs of his family. Most men, tied down to the daily problems of earning their bread, could not give their strength and total devotion to outside causes, such as the ones Louis had made his own.

"All the more reason to work hard and get something done," Louis yawned as he considered the coming day. He pulled out his pocket watch by its golden chain, saw that it was late, and prepared for the night.

Before he turned out the light Louis took a small slip of paper out of his wallet. Many years ago his friend Sam Warren had copied a verse by the Greek dramatist Euripides onto this paper and sent it to Louis. Now, dear Sam had gone from this earth too. Tonight he had been much on Louis's mind.

"Go forth, my son, and help," read the last line of the poem. It had been a guide to Louis for a long time. As he closed his eyes Louis wondered how many occasions were yet to come when the poem would serve him as an inspiration.

TEN

The governor of the state of New Jersey had a summer home in Sea Girt, on the coast. Here the Wilson family had come to relax and here Woodrow Wilson had received the news of his presidential nomination. Now the Governor's Cottage was no longer a vacation retreat, but the humming headquarters where the candidate worked on his plans for the coming election. It was to this house that Louis Brandeis came for his first private meeting with Woodrow Wilson in August 1912.

As the car bringing Louis approached, the lean, aristocratic man wearing rimless eyeglasses appeared on the spacious front porch. Governor Wilson had made his acceptance speech from here a few weeks ago, and the lawn and shrubbery still bore the marks of the throng of people who had pushed their way close to hear.

Woodrow Wilson stretched out a welcoming hand. "Your visit gives me great pleasure," he told Louis, "for I have been very much cheered and reassured by your support of my campaign."

"Thank you, Mr. Governor," replied Louis. "I have said publicly that I feel your nomination is one of the most encouraging events in American history. You possess qualities of leadership that this country needs. I am here to assure you of my assistance, whenever that may be required."

Mrs. Ellen Wilson, the governor's lady, had arranged a simple luncheon, and as they sat down to the meal Louis became a witness to the devoted family life of the Wilsons. How very much like my own home this is, Louis felt instinctively, and thought of Alice.

Afterward the two men talked. The former president of Princeton University and the attorney from Boston discovered each other that day.

As the hours passed they moved to a rear porch, where they watched the sea and relaxed in white wicker chairs. They planned the important campaign months ahead.

Louis had heard Woodrow Wilson speak to crowds. He knew the persuasive magic with which Wilson could win masses of people. This was not always the case when a person faced him alone, people had told Louis. Then he could be haughty and impatient, especially if the visitor did not agree with Wilson's views.

During the long afternoon the governor and Louis found that a spark had passed between them. The one big thing Wilson needed was a campaign issue, something to stir the people. Brandeis could supply it.

"The major point of my campaign will be a cause close to your heart, dear Brandeis," the nominee told him. "I know your splendid record in the anti-monopoly fight. It is only fitting that we should map out this part of the platform together. It is what you have been working for these many years."

Louis was pleased that the discussion between him and the candidate went well. Governor Wilson concentrated as Louis explained to him how a strong antitrust law would keep down business monopolies.

"Exactly," Wilson agreed. "This will be a basic issue of my New Freedom concept."

Louis answered questions, he produced figures, he shared his notes with the attentive Wilson. Louis was enthusiastic and completely at ease.

"You know, Mr. Brandeis, how I agree with you wholeheartedly on this question of competition in business. I have learned much from you today. Could we count on you to do some talking on that subject in the larger, more populated areas of our country?"

Louis nodded understandingly. "I can't refuse you, sir. Battling the privileged few who seek to control the many is an essential part of my life. Explaining the topic of trusts is a favorite with me. I will discuss it at length with anyone who will listen."

Wilson rose from his chair. Cordially he touched Louis's arm. "Brandeis, I want you to know I am deeply grateful. You are not only one of the busiest men in the country, but also one of the most help-ful."

6. *Justice Brandeis and his wife, Alice, on a stroll near their Washington home in later years*

"I am pleased at the chance, sir."

"What has taken place here this afternoon will reflect great credit on you. I do not intend to forget your enormous assistance to me, but I must tell you that I consider this to be only the beginning. I hope there will be many more meetings between us."

"I am certain there will be, governor."

"Keep me supplied with those papers of yours. I'm certain they will provide the backbone for many a campaign speech."

Louis laughed. "Some say paperwork is my weakness, that I turn out too much of it. I hope this won't become your opinion, sir."

Wilson looked wistful for a moment as he said, "With these constant hordes of people who now walk in on our life at all hours, I often miss the scholar's solitude, the quiet moments when there were only my books and I. But politics has changed all that."

The car arrived to escort Louis back to the station. There was time for a last handshake. Then Louis walked down the steps of the Governor's Cottage. He knew he had made a friend.

"But I do not want a cabinet post," Louis protested to his friends, who were angered when Woodrow Wilson announced the names of his new cabinet members just two days before his inauguration in March 1913.

"Louis, after all, you have been practically the backbone of Wilson's campaign. These many months in which you have worked in every possible way to help the president win should be rewarded."

"Those of us who know you well," said another friend, "have seen how really devoted you have been in your efforts. We know how your family has had to be without you while you traveled over half the country on speaking engagements. Your friends, too, have been deprived of your company. Think of the many nights you worked late on speeches for the president-elect. If it hadn't been for your writings, the people of our country would still not know what Wilson's 'New Freedom' campaign was all about. You sold him and his campaign to the people."

"I won't deny I worked hard," replied Louis. "No political campaign is mounted without work. But you must be fair. You have heard all the same rumors which have come to my ears: that Woodrow Wilson wanted me as attorney general in his cabinet, but that his advisors were against it."

"That's exactly the reason why we are so perturbed, Louis. If he wanted you—and the whole city of Washington is buzzing with talk that he had you in mind for three different cabinet posts—why didn't he insist on it? Why did he let himself be talked out of it?"

In the midst of so much consternation Louis alone was calm. "It's my radical reputation, I suppose, which frightens the politicians," he shrugged. "I am the bad boogeyman to big business. Now all my former opponents can have their day influencing the president against me. President Wilson should not start out a new administration with a handicap like the Brandeis name attached to it."

"Your attitude proves you to be a big man, Louis, but. . . ."

"Look"—Louis stood in the center of his parlor, holding up his hands to indicate that he wanted no further discussion—"I am not perturbed in the least. I have done my best for President Wilson's election, and it pleases me that he was successful. But if I have no political post to restrain me, I am all the happier for it. It means that I will have more time now to pursue my other projects. I need energy for some of the big antitrust trials still ahead of me. I want to do some writing. And, of course, the Zionist cause now needs my help."

To his friends Louis seemed contented and willing to overlook the many prejudices and pressures President Woodrow Wilson had faced when he wanted to include his friend Brandeis in his official government family. Louis knew that the president wanted him. He also knew that he would continue to serve Wilson with his advice and guidance. He might even be more closely listened to just because he was a man free of political ties who wanted nothing in return for his services.

But he was saddened by the cabinet episode. Saddened because he knew a great many things were still needed to set America aright.

Louis was convinced that it was not only the politicians who had kept him out of the cabinet. He was a reformer, yes. But the country had been swept by the spirit of reform, and citizens were responding to the causes sponsored by men like La Follette, Theodore Roosevelt, Wilson, and others. Wilson had been elected on the basis of his reform platform. Why, then, did the name Brandeis draw fire?

"It's the big business interests who have really won the day," he confided to Alice when they were alone late at night.

She shook her head sadly, not giving voice to complaint.

"Anyone who tangles with men of the New Haven Railroad or the United Shoe Machinery Company pays a price for his impudence," said Louis.

"But, my goodness, how wrong this is!" she exclaimed. "After so many years one expects more enlightenment in men of government."

"There is a glimmer, but it will take more time to spread. Truthfully, I am concerned that President Wilson will not be able to assert himself sufficiently within his own administration. He is too fine a man to be caught up in political machinations. So much needs to be set straight in our domestic situation right here, but now he has to worry about the European war scare, too."

"I can't believe Europe will get into war, can you, Louis?"

"I certainly hope there will be no strife. It might involve the United States."

When Alice went upstairs for the night, Louis sat down at his desk and began writing letters. First he shared the day's news with Alfred in Louisville. Then he wrote to a friend: "I am inclined to think that the situation as it is, is best. There is a wide field of usefulness for a *public* private citizen."

He sat back in his desk chair to read over what he had written. Thoughtfully, he nodded as if in agreement. Then he switched off the lamp in the small, book-lined study and climbed the steps to the upper floor. It *had* been an eventful day.

One morning soon after, Alice packed Louis's travel bags again. As she folded his shirts neatly to fit the suitcase, she worried. Louis had been looking tired and thin lately. He was doing too much, she thought. He was still contesting the New Haven Railroad in strenuous court sessions, and now he was starting a cross-country tour to lecture in behalf of Zionism.

"Take care of yourself, dear," she said to Louis when he was ready to leave the house. Downstairs two men from the local Zionist organization waited to take him to the railroad station. They wanted to give him last-minute information which Louis was to use in his speeches.

"After all these years of marriage I am still a lucky man," Louis smiled at Alice upstairs, "to have you do all these things for me." He pointed to the closed suitcases. "People are always saying it's amazing how much work I can get done during a day. They don't know what an efficient part you play in my planning."

And then he was gone. Alice peeked out between the crisply starched white curtains of her bedroom window and saw the open car leave 114

Mount Vernon Street. Her husband, seated between two steadily talking men, turned and waved her a parting greeting.

The audiences who came to hear the eminent jurist Louis Dembitz Brandeis talk to them about the Zionist cause were rarely disappointed in their speaker. True, he did not attempt to spellbind them. Nor did he use his dry wit on them, as he had been known to do in the courtroom.

Louis told the groups, the clubs, and the religious organizations his honest thoughts on the development of the Jewish people.

"Self-respect," he said as he stood at the lectern in one hall after another. "We as Jews must regain our self-respect. The servile manner, the submissiveness to persecution must be outgrown. And Zionism is the answer to that."

He told them about the Jewish students at the University of Vienna who had been the object of jeers and blows by their fellow students.

"But Zionism gave them courage. They formed associations and learned athletic drill and fencing. Insult was requited with insult, and presently the best fencers of the fighting German corps found that Zionist students could gash cheeks quite as effectively as any Teuton, and that the Jews were in a fair way to become the best swordsmen of the university."

Time was growing short, he said. The Jews of Poland and nearby countries were threatened and suffering untold miseries daily. The answer was simple. If Jewry was to be saved, the way must be opened for immigration to Palestine. Turkey, which held territorial rights to the land of Palestine, must be petitioned to give up some of its area to allow Jews to resettle there. The funds to start industry which would give work to the new settlers must come from America. These were the three practical steps to accomplish a miracle.

People listened to him attentively. Often his speeches swayed men who had come to the meeting prepared to be against Zionism, who felt that the establishment of a Jewish homeland was not a problem for an American Jew to ponder. But when they heard Louis speak, his idealism and enthusiasm won them over.

"If a big man like Brandeis thinks Palestine can be made into a future home for Jews, maybe there is something to it," they said to each other after Louis had talked.

"This is no dreamer, after all. Brandeis is a hard-headed lawyer who knows his facts. He wouldn't lend his name to a cause he didn't fully believe in."

Louis was glad when people asked questions after his speeches. It proved he had stirred them to think about matters. It bore out a fact which had been disturbing him for some time. In his travels he had many occasions to meet thinking people, people who had definite views regarding Jewish life in America. They asked intelligent questions and offered intelligent solutions to problems of the day.

But Louis knew that in the big decisions which affected Jews in America, the average Jew did not have a part. It was as if he did not exist. For the deciding voice of the Jewish community was that of the rich, influential man, the leader who presumed to speak for everyone, but in actuality spoke only for his own interests.

Louis had discussed this imbalance with Rabbi Stephen Wise, his coworker in Zionist affairs and his friend.

"It is as if we were still in the archaic system of Europe, where the court Jew—*Hofjude*—played go-between for the Jewish community and the ruling powers. When the community wanted a favor, some improvement of their deplorable living conditions perhaps or an easing of the strict laws governing them, it turned to the *Hofjude*. Most of the time the local duke or prince was obligated to the Jew who served as his moneylender, so he had to see him and listen to his requests. But, as you are well aware, some of our well-to-do friends have carried this arrangement into the present day."

Stephen Wise knew well that Louis was right. He had had a few experiences of his own with wealthy, influential men who did not share his ideas of democratic living. So he nodded as Louis continued, "There are now three million Jews living in America. It is certainly wrong that they have no voice of their own. No one speaks for them, for surely our philanthropic Jewish millionaires do not have the masses in mind when they say, 'Zionism is not for Americans' or 'It will arouse anti-Semitism if too much emphasis is placed on Jewish things in public.' "

Stephen Wise was in full agreement, too, when Louis explained his theory that American Jews should be democratically organized to reach their own decisions and play their full part in the conduct of Jewish affairs. For, as Louis so aptly put it to him, "Is a man less qualified to have proper judgment because he is not wealthy?"

Now, when Louis talked to audiences throughout the country, he often mentioned the idea that a group of people living in a democracy should perform as citizens, and the only working way this could be achieved would be by a representative method.

"Elect delegates from among you," he stressed, "and send them to a congress where they can discuss issues confronting present-day Jews. After that a vote can be taken democratically, and only then will you have a truly representative point of view."

When Louis broached the subject of a congress of American Jews to his lecture groups, it often went through his mind that once again he was fighting "bigness." Only this time it was among his own people. It took courage to speak out as he did, but there was no other way. He believed this just as he believed that the greatness of America lay in the right of her people to rule themselves.

Dave, the little cutter from the East Side who had been his guide during the garment strike days, had said to Louis: "Only by organizing can we pull ourselves out of the rut." He had talked about labor unions at the time, but it struck Louis frequently during his constant travels that it applied to the emergence of Jewish thought and action as well.

ELEVEN

All the fears Louis had expressed on his lecture tour were justified within a few months. In August 1914 war broke out in Europe. Now his concern for the Jews trapped in the war zone became a consuming anxiety. The vast distress of these homeless people spurred him to work on plans to save them.

August, a month usually spent vacationing with Alice and his daughters, was devoted to seclusion in his study instead. There in the small room he sat, surrounded by papers and books which provided the facts he needed.

Alice tiptoed in from time to time, depositing snacks on the corner of the table, not disturbing him while he was so deeply absorbed in studying the reports.

When occasionally he did look up and smile at her, she did not want to nag him about overworking in the summer heat. Wasn't it silly to act like a fussing wife when Louis was so earnestly engaged in such serious work?

"Thanks," he said in a rare moment of relaxation, "for acting like Alice and thinking unselfish thoughts."

And Alice, who now knew that Louis had guessed her thoughts all along, was glad she had remained silent.

A few days after the outbreak of the war, she ushered Jacob de Haas into the little study. He wasted no time in telling Louis why he had come.

"I want your permission to suggest your name as head of the committee which will now have to run practically the whole Zionist movement."

Louis tilted his head questioningly.

"Surely, dear Louis, you are aware that with the outbreak of hostilities we have become cut off from the main Zionist center in Berlin?"

"Yes," Louis nodded slowly, "I had realized that."

"This means that all leadership must now come from America." De Haas emphasized each word distinctly.

Louis said nothing and de Haas continued, "There is no person better equipped for this position than you, dear friend." Then he paused, awaiting an answer.

"You've prepared this moment well, Jacob. Isn't it strange the way fate has given you the push to make it come true?"

"From our first meeting together, I knew that you—you, Louis—were to be the one who must carry on Herzl's leadership. Now I know how right my intuition was that afternoon you walked me to the train in South Yarmouth and I asked, 'And what do you think of Zionism, Mr. Brandeis?'"

"I have seen many railroad tracks since that day."

"Yes, no one has brought the issue of Zionism before the American Jew the way you have, Louis. Your name has become identified with the movement. It is you the people know. It is to you they will look for leadership. For that is the heart of the problem now. With European Zionism stopped by the war, it is not only the movement that is endangered, but the survival of the Jewish people is at stake. Indeed, I am speaking of the welfare of seven-tenths of the Jewish people."

"You are proposing a challenging task for me, Jacob."

"No person alive is more capable of it than you are. The day will come when world Zionism may turn to you for leadership. And if the Jewish people in Europe are prepared to accept a leader who lives so far away, then I will say, too, you are the man for the job."

"You are looking into the future. The urgency is here now. You may propose my name to your committee, Jacob."

As the new chairman of the Provisional Executive Committee for General Zionist Affairs, Louis met with the 150 delegates who had elected him.

He stood in the place of honor at the speakers' table and bowed his head as applause of the delegates filled the room. Then he raised his right hand, asking for silence.

"Friends," he addressed them, "it seems strange to have spent so many long years of my life separated from Jewish concerns and ignorant of most of them, and now to be before you as head of this committee, which has such a vital function in the progress of our people.

"But I have learned many things in recent years. The time is right for us to begin work on the rebirth of the Jewish homeland. This is the task before us. I know it is work important to us all. Help me to do my part, and I will work out proposals that will get us started."

The morning meeting ended, and the delegates were trickling out of the hall, but Louis asked the executive officers to stay and listen to his plans.

Summer heat flooded through partially opened windows. Soon the men took off their coats, wiping their brows as they continued to listen to Louis. It was not to be a short meeting. Their speaker did not seem to mind his discomfort, or theirs.

In late afternoon the skies darkened and the heat in the hall hung over them like a wet sheet. Still their chairman talked. His eyes focused on each man in the room, and each one felt that he had personally been addressed and was inspired to new energy.

"What we do here may affect the welfare of the youth of Israel, and that of generations still unborn," Louis said to them.

Finally, thunder broke outside and the heavy rain washed the New York sidewalks clean. The tension of the delegates was released, and they forgot time and place as they settled down to work, however long it might take.

It may have occurred to some of the men that in their own way they were engaged in a project not unlike that of a small group of men who had met on a similarly hot day in Philadelphia in the summer of 1776. The work that was done in the state of Pennsylvania influenced the future of the country soon to be born. The planning now going on in the meeting hall of a New York hotel might move another new land into life. They—the men in shirtsleeves—might well be presiding over the birth of a new nation.

"I wish to make an announcement," said the chairman. "As you know, the outbreak of the war has seriously endangered the crops planted in our already established colonies in Palestine. Not only are the fields suffering from the lack of tending, but our own *chalutzim,* the pioneers who have started these settlements, are in need of food and money. It is therefore with great appreciation and delight that I want to tell you of the generous donation made by Mr. Nathan Straus of this city. Mr. Straus's gift will start a campaign for the relief of our pioneers."

Eleven men, the entire committee, stood up to applaud the news. Then they continued their work, their meeting lasting through most of the night.

When they met again the following morning, Louis introduced a new topic.

"It is with great concern that we view the day when the war ends and the Jews put before the Great Powers the question of establishing a homeland. Who shall speak for us? As you gentlemen are aware, there is no one organization which truly represents all American Jewry. Why?"

Then Louis told the assembled group of his recent troubled thoughts on the lack of unity in American Jewish affairs.

"American Jews have come of age. They can be trusted to use the tools of democracy in their own problems, as in the problems of their country. So let there be a democratic way of expression for us. When it comes to the decisions governing our people, let us make them in a way befitting the dignity of a democratic system.

"Those who have spoken for us in the past have done it because it benefited them to be the leaders and spokesmen for the American Jew. Those who professed to voice our opinions did it because it gave them prestige and standing. They took it upon themselves to be the leaders and the spokesmen, for none of us ever elected them to that task.

"But the age of Jewish anonymity is gone. We need no longer be self-abasing and plead for tolerance. Those who advised us to be meek were wrong. They were moved by that great fear of anti-Semitism which always hangs over any Jewish undertaking.

"We have the right and the self-respect to campaign for those equal rights which belong to all Americans. Let us start by handling our own affairs in a united, democratic fashion.

"Within a short time I am going to propose to all major Jewish organizations in our country that we merge into one joint body, duly elected. This will be an American Jewish Congress, the truly representative voice of us all before the world."

That autumn Louis and his friend Rabbi Wise visited the White House together. Woodrow Wilson had received an unspeakably great blow when death claimed his beloved wife, Ellen, in late summer. Facing all the important problems of his office that fall was very difficult for him. He saw few visitors. But Louis and Rabbi Wise were his friends, and he knew them to be devoted family men sympathetic to his grief.

"I know you have come to discuss the Jewish homeland with me," he greeted them when they were shown to a sitting room near his office. "Because this is an important topic to you and to me, I have asked Secretary Daniels to join us in our talk. As you know, Mr. Daniels has been very sympathetic to the cause," the president added.

Rabbi Wise and Secretary of the Navy Josephus Daniels shook hands. Then, at the invitation of President Wilson, they sat down on a small sofa opposite the president's chair, while Louis settled down at the president's right.

"My friend Brandeis sees me often, and always when I'm in the midst of difficulties. He has come to think of me as needing his help. I am glad to have the chance to be of help to him or to a cause dear to his heart," the president opened the talk. "Tell me what I can do."

"Mr. President, it is of immeasurable value to us Zionists to have your support. Can we count on you to back us up when the time comes to make our demands before a council of nations?" asked Louis.

"Are you speaking of demands for land?" the president questioned. Louis nodded. "Of course, this is a point which must wait until a peace treaty is under discussion," Wilson said, "but I happily give you my promise now to support your every demand."

"We are deeply grateful, sir, but how do you believe the Allies—Britain and France—will feel toward the idea?"

"I am inclined to think that Britain and France will agree with the United States and back the establishment of a Jewish Palestine. But let me suggest to you, friend, that you contact the British and French ambassadors and put the matter before them while they are here in Washington. You will be doing important groundwork that should prepare for the day when the matter can be worked out openly."

"Your advice is valuable, Mr. President. Rabbi Wise and I shall be busy doing that in the months to come. In the meantime. . . ." Louis looked at Rabbi Wise, who had listened patiently to all the discussion that went on between the president and Louis. The president looked too, and guessed that the topic of Palestine had not yet been exhausted.

"Mr. President," said Rabbi Wise now, "you have been so burdened in recent months that you may not have been aware of a problem which besets our Palestinian colonies now that war has hit them. The settlers who have gotten the desert to bloom are now starving themselves, and their crops have been drying up. They need help desperately. The Zionist Organization has collected money to start a campaign, but the need is so great and the obstacles nearly overwhelming."

"Daniels, that is your department," the president said, turning to the secretary of the navy. "See what you can do to get some shiploads of food and supplies to those settlers. I know it makes you happy to do these errands of mercy."

Then he faced Louis again. "Dear Brandeis, I was glad to learn that you are now the leader of the Zionist movement in this country. In fact, it makes me doubly glad, for not only am I strongly in favor of restoring the Jewish people to their ancient home, but I am delighted to have a friend of mine at the head of the crusade."

He rose and shook hands with both his visitors.

"Mr. President, the Jewish people have in you a great friend," Rabbi Wise told Woodrow Wilson.

"I feel especially blessed to be the occupant of this house at a time when the fate of the Jewish people depends on the support of its friends," answered the president of the United States.

As Secretary Daniels and Rabbi Wise crossed the threshold of the presidential parlor, Woodrow Wilson touched Louis's shoulder with his hand. "Stay a moment. There is something I wish to say to you, friend."

Louis stopped still and looked into the president's weary face. The others had walked down the corridor and were no longer within hearing.

"I was unwise sometime ago in a decision which concerned you."

Louis looked down. He knew he was blushing, but he remained silent.

"I want you to know that when the next occasion arises, I shall listen to no counsel but my own."

For the second time in a few minutes Louis shook the hand which was offered him. "Thank you, Mr. President."

It was all he could say.

It was very hot in Boston on Independence Day of 1915. All day the sun had brightened picnics and outings. Now, in late afternoon, the sidewalks in the inner heart of the market area still reflected the warmth they had received earlier. But the good citizens of Boston were not deterred by anything as trivial as a heat wave. The doors of imposing Faneuil Hall opened early to receive the crowds into its historical chamber for that yearly event, the Fourth of July oration.

The printed program read: *Mr. Louis D. Brandeis, Speaker.*

The curious and the concerned came from all sections of the city to listen. The ladies from the Back Bay and Beacon Hill, white-gloved and well-behaved, attended the event much as their eminent ancestors had done for many years.

"A bit unusual, isn't it, for the city to ask a newcomer to Boston to speak?" they whispered among themselves. "After all, it *is* such a traditional thing, this oration."

The men of learning—the lawyers and doctors and teachers—who knew of the work Brandeis had done in their city and state were anxious to hear what he thought of the matter which affected them all during these days of political jitters and fears.

"Does he believe there'll be war? Will we get into it?" they asked themselves.

The workers and laborers from East Boston and the West End had brought along their families to see in person the man who was helping them toward better working conditions. They came prepared to applaud and cheer noisily whenever their champion said anything that appealed to them.

All who sat in the warm plush seats of Faneuil Hall that day were aware that the speaker's topic, "True Americanism," was just right for this hall, called by many the real Cradle of Liberty. For wasn't it here that early colonists had held many of their meetings to protest British rule and to make their own decisions regarding their future?

"I want to explain to you what they mean to me, these rights of life, liberty, and the pursuit of happiness," said Louis, a tall Lincoln-like figure, from the large stage. "Life, in this connection, should mean living, not existing."

And the wives of the workers in the auditorium thought of their large families, the small paychecks their men brought home, and the huge task of "making do."

"Liberty," their speaker said, "should mean freedom in things industrial as well as political."

Unpleasant images of union organizers being beaten, lost jobs, and lockouts by their employers traveled through the minds of the laborers present.

"Happiness," said Louis, pointing a slender hand at them all, "should include, among other things, that satisfaction which can come only through the full development and use of one's faculties."

His first love was America. This was clear to everyone who heard him speak. All the themes dear to his heart were in this speech: pleas for shorter hours and higher wages for the workingman, the right of women to vote, an open door to immigration.

All the causes to which he has given his time and his strength during his public career, thought Alice, sitting in the audience with both her daughters. *Not many men have done as much as Louis.*

There is in Americanism a precious and unique feature, Louis told his audience, which is different from all other forms of democracy as practiced in other lands. This is the ideal of inclusive brotherhood. And he asked them to guard this ideal.

"Each race or people, like each individual, has the right and the duty to develop. Only through such development will high civilization be attained. Equal opportunity is the key. Equal opportunity is the basis of international as well as national justice. And only when all peoples have these rights and these opportunities will there be permanent peace in the world."

TWELVE

President Wilson chose January 28, 1916, to inform the Senate that he had appointed Louis D. Brandeis as associate justice of the Supreme Court of the United States.

On that Friday in January Louis had business in Washington. He had left his home after dinner on Thursday to board an overnight train which was to take him to a full day's work at the Justice Department.

"I hope you'll have a good day in Washington tomorrow," Alice said, handing him a second cup of coffee, and Louis decided to linger a few minutes more at the dinner table with her.

"Strange that at this hour only three people are in on the secret. I feel as if I'm about to set off an explosion."

"Oh, never fear—there'll be much noise soon," responded Alice. "This is one matter about which everyone in the country will have his say."

Poor Alice, Louis thought, *until this thing is over she and the girls will have a difficult time. They will take the slurs and insinuations much more seriously than I. It'll be harder on them. . . . They will try to hide their disturbed feelings from me.*

"My dear, we'll have much excitement from now on—" he started, when Alice suddenly giggled.

"Well, dear, you are certainly beginning your retirement with a big celebration," she said.

She hasn't giggled like this since she was a young girl, Louis thought. He could tell the excitement of the coming day had begun to work on Alice.

Yes, they *had* talked about his retirement in recent months. It was pleasant to ponder over all the things they would do together once the pressures of his public work ceased. But it was a dream now.

Louis reached over the table to Alice's hands, folded in front of her. "I would have liked that . . . to retire and to have some time with you and the girls. Now that Susan's out of college and Elizabeth will be soon, we could have done things together more . . . enjoy ourselves as we used to during August vacations."

Alice patted his hand. "But now . . ." she said.

"But now," Louis continued for her, "I'm glad I'm not retiring. Now that the justiceship has come about. For I know that my work is not done. Ever since the cabinet episode I have known that big business is still running the show behind the scenes, despite the antitrust bills and other laws. I may have done a little bit of good, but now there is an even larger area for me to work in. The court is a challenge."

"They'll crucify you," she answered.

"What more can they say? It's all been said in the last ten years."

"They'll organize campaigns against you, vilify you wherever they can," she replied.

"Nothing new. We're used to it, aren't we, dear?"

Louis looked at his wife. How long had her hair been sprinkled with gray?

"Alice, these things are hard on a man's family, I know. But you must have no fear about me. I am fortunate. I have peace of mind. I can take the outcome, whatever it will be."

"It will be a dirty fight, Louis, and a long one."

"There'll be name-calling, yes. Slander and anti-Semitism, too—only the anti-Semitism will go underground. No senator is going to permit his name to be linked with prejudice if he can help it. Too many votes depend on it. A man needs a liberal, clean record to wave before the voters back home."

"Then it'll take other forms. They'll disguise the anti-Semitism and use other words—words like radical, socialist—anything to frighten a public not familiar enough with the facts to see through the smears."

Louis pushed back his chair and rose from the table. "Yes, my big business friends will again stir the witches' brew designed to drown me. But this time the president will persist. You'll see."

Alice watched Louis bundle himself into his heavy overcoat against the wintry night air. She held his hat while he closed the coat buttons.

"We mustn't forget the many on *your* side. The

labor leaders, the workers, the shopkeepers, all the 'little men on Main Street.' They all know what it means to have a Brandeis on the bench of the Supreme Court guarding their interests."

"Ah, yes, the radical from Boston," responded Louis, now pulling on his gloves, and they both laughed.

"Don't worry too much, my dear. If the Senate votes in accordance with the president's wishes, we'll have enough support to get me through."

"I hope you're right, Louis. I surely hope so."

The next day as he sat at a paper-strewn desk in the Justice Department, Louis glanced up at the big clock mounted on the painted wall. Down the street, on Constitution Avenue, the Senate was now meeting in full session. Sometime during the hour the name of Louis Dembitz Brandeis would be read aloud in the high-domed chamber. Then the battle would begin.

Louis sensed that this would be the last hour of political calm in the Capitol until the issue was settled. Whether the Senate confirmed the president's nomination or not, the arguments would be strong and fierce. Woodrow Wilson knew this too.

Just a few days earlier he had sent for Louis and told him he wished to elect him to the vacancy on the nation's highest court of law. Louis had agreed to accept.

"It will be a fight," the president had said to him, "but I mean to see it through."

Then, without consulting a single senator, the president sent the name of his choice to Capitol Hill. It was a completely unusual move. By custom, leading senators knew who the president's nominee was, perhaps even advised him on his choice. Not so this time.

President Wilson remembered too well what had happened the last time he wanted Louis Brandeis to have an official position.

I think I had best stay out of Washington for the duration, Louis reflected. *No need to be in the limelight. I must watch myself with the press too. Keep quiet. Enough will be said about me as it is.*

The next morning newspapers screamed the President's appointment to all parts of the nation.

WILSON SHOCKS CONGRESS BY NAMING BRANDEIS FOR THE UNITED STATES SUPREME COURT

said *The New York Sun* in a three-column heading. Following was a smaller headline reading:

He's First Jew Ever Picked For Bench.

The secret was out. The fight had begun. It was time to settle in for the siege.

Now that he was back in Boston for the length of the confirmation fight, Louis went to his law office every day. It was not strange to be spending time at his own desk again. It was a comfortable, familiar feeling to read his mail, sitting in his well-worn black leather chair. Occasionally Louis swiveled the chair around to look at the world through the window facing Devonshire Street. Here it had all started . . . in the one-room office shared with Sam Warren. From here he had conducted his law cases, then begun his public service career now reaching its peak. The friendships of a lifetime, and the enemies as well. . . .

There was a knock on the door.

"Good morning, Mr. Brandeis," said Alice Grady, his longtime secretary, as she brought in the mail.

Letters from every part of the country were finding their way to him since the nomination had hit the newspapers. It was amazing: from every segment of the population he received letters which said, "In you, Louis Brandeis, we have found our defender." They came from students, poor people, labor union officials, and political thinkers of the Progressive movement.

Recently he had traveled to New York for a special meeting of the New York arbitration board of the dress industry. This was the organization he had helped to create during the garment workers' struggle. Neither employer nor worker had forgotten how much they owed to Louis's mediation during those bitter days.

They congratulated Louis and told him how right the president had been to promote their chairman to a justiceship in the highest court of the land. It warmed him to have their support.

From the stacks of letters heaped on his desk, Louis picked one to read again. A judge in North Dakota urged him to action.

"By your zeal for the common good," the judge wrote, "you have created powerful enemies. They will do their utmost to defeat your confirmation in the Senate, but they must not be permitted to succeed. . . . Please do not allow the reluctance which every man of honor feels against defending his own life to prevent your meeting the issue. You owe it to your country as well as to yourself."

Thoughtfully Louis stared at the letter. If he could not do it, perhaps his law partners would battle for him. It was boring to sit back. He could not meet the attacks of his opponents as he used to in his own courtroom days. And to have others do the fighting for him . . . he didn't like that a bit. But. . . .

If he spoke out in his own behalf, he would appear anxious, eager for the position. This was not being true to himself. Louis Brandeis never took time to defend himself. It was up to his adversaries to prove the virtue of their position. Besides, it was against President Wilson's wishes that his candidate for such a high office appear to answer charges against him publicly.

Immediately after the nomination, the Senate had selected a subcommittee of five men. They were to investigate the many charges which arose against the confirmation of Louis Brandeis.

The senators received numerous letters very similar in language and content, all containing accusations against the nominee. Quickly the committee members understood that an organized mail campaign was under way to prevent the confirmation of Brandeis.

The hateful letters came from businessmen and lawyers who had lost cases to Louis Brandeis during his days of the United Shoe Machinery and New Haven Railroad fights. But important men lent their names and energies to this distasteful cause, too.

"Let us speak out for you," many of Louis's friends and associates said to him. "We can gather petitions endorsing you and write letters to the White House and to the Senate countering that vicious campaign against you."

Especially unhappy were those friends who had been disappointed the first time Louis's name had been considered—and then dropped—for the cabinet post. They could not allow a similar episode to recur.

When sixty lawyers from Boston petitioned the Senate against confirmation, led by the president of Harvard University himself, great anger filled Harvard students.

"Is this the way to treat one of the school's most illustrious graduates?" they asked. "Louis Brandeis has brought only honor to the law school during his career."

Jewish members of the Bar Association wanted to take action, as did the labor group from New York. "We'll have mass meetings promoting Louis Brandeis as *our* choice," they suggested.

"No, no. It wouldn't be wise at this time," Louis declined gratefully.

The hearings of the subcommittee continued into March, April, and then May. Witness after witness appeared. Brandeis supporters became restless. Louis's law partners now spent their days in Washington, sitting in on the meetings. They defended charges against Louis with facts which he sent them from Boston. No one had expected the confirmation to take this long. No end to the hearings was in sight.

"If the president wants you on the Supreme Court, he should make this known to the Senate in definite terms. He knew this would be a difficult fight. Now is the time for him to back you up," said the Brandeis advisors.

Then the Senate received a letter from President Wilson. "I am profoundly interested in the confirmation of the appointment," wrote the president.

The report of the subcommittee, which had now been submitted to the Senate, proved, said the president, how unfounded were the charges made against Louis Brandeis.

"I myself looked into them three years ago when I desired to make Mr. Brandeis a member of my cabinet," continued Woodrow Wilson's letter, "and found that they proceeded for the most part from those who hated Mr. Brandeis because he had refused to be serviceable to them in the promotion of their own selfish interests, and from those whom they had prejudiced. . . . I knew from direct personal knowledge of the man what I was doing when I named him for the highest and most responsible tribunal of the Nation."

During these days of heated headlines, news of the Brandeis confirmation battle vied with accounts of the approaching entanglement in the European war.

From the shelter of his study, Louis worked for

the one cause which still needed him sorely. He had retired from every other activity while awaiting news from Washington, but the Zionist movement continued to have his strong, active support.

On March 26, 1916, in Philadelphia, a great preliminary meeting of the American Jewish Congress had taken place. The group had chosen Louis D. Brandeis as its honorary president. Louis was heartened. He and his friends had finally brought their brainchild into the world.

On a blustery Sunday afternoon in late March, Rabbi Stephen Wise walked up the crunchy, snowy driveway of the Brandeis home. Louis had been watching for him from his study window upstairs. He smiled happily when the big, granite-featured man flung his arms around him and announced in ringing tones, "I bring you the greetings of the first American Jewish Congress, Mr. President."

What a source of strength he has always been . . . this giant in build and mind, thought Louis, regarding his friend fondly.

"I was with you in thought every step of the way," Louis answered. "I wanted very much to be in Philadelphia."

"We knew that. We also knew that now you can't be publicly involved in anything but this nomination. But it was thrilling. . . . Oh, Louis, my friend . . . this gathering would have made your heart swell."

"Tell me." Louis helped his friend with his coat, anxiously studying the rabbi's mobile face, still glowing from the cold outside.

"Oh, I will. . . . That's why I came, Louis."

Together they mounted the steps to the upstairs study, where Louis cautioned his friend to take care, for there were books arranged in heaps and stacks everywhere—on the desk, on the arms of a chair, on the floor.

"Always working, aren't you?" said Wise. The modest room seemed crowded with this radiant man in its center.

"I heard your opening speech was excellent, Stephen."

"It was an inspiring group. Imagine, we had this large banquet hall packed with people. There were three hundred and sixty-seven delegates from every major Jewish organization in the country. They had come to *do* things, big things. And to act *together*. Here was unity for the first time. Oh, Louis, it was exciting."

Rabbi Wise had gotten up and was walking back and forth across the little room, his arms spread out, gesturing. Louis could almost see the scene the rabbi was trying to re-create for him.

"To think our dream has finally come true," Louis mused. "Well, at least the first part of the dream—the hard work is yet ahead."

"But, Louis, think of the achievement! Never before has a group of this size sat down together, decided together, and voted together for one cause . . . to help its fellow man."

"The cause is urgent. It had to be like this."

"Now that we have the American Jewish Congress almost on its feet, what about you, Louis?"

"You mean if I'm confirmed for the court?"

"Yes, will you be able to continue with us?"

"I intend to, Stephen. I may be forced to resign the honorary chairmanship. If I am to be a justice of the Supreme Court, I want to do my job whole-heartedly. But I hope to continue to advise and assist the Zionist cause and the congress."

"Thank God," Rabbi Wise breathed fervently.

"Stephen...." Louis leaned back in his chair and toyed with a small letter opener on his desk. "Stephen, have you ever thought how strange it is for us to be friends and co-workers in behalf of Judaism, you a rabbi and I a Jew who has never attended synagogue in his life?"

"Yes, I have, Louis. Quite often, to be truthful. I have also come to a conclusion about it. Would you like to hear it?"

Louis looked up into the flashing eyes of his friend, who now stood beside his desk, towering over him.

"A rabbi, any rabbi, wants to see the heritage of Judaism passed down and preserved from one generation to the next. The inspiration and learning received in the House of God is the best means of transmitting this heritage.

"Though you were never an observant Jew, your every deed is proof that the Judaic tradition is strong and secure within you. There is something more. Perhaps a rabbi can spot this more easily than others." Louis stirred in his chair and Stephen Wise continued. "There is a quality of *kedushah* about you—a holiness—which is felt by every person whose life yours touches. You are blessed, Louis, and," Rabbi Wise added softly, "you have passed the blessing on to others."

The faith that Louis held in the decent legal processes of the American system of democracy helped him win his most important case. On June 1, 1916, after four months of hearings and debates, the Senate voted for the confirmation of Louis D. Brandeis as associate justice of the Supreme Court by a count of 47 to 22.

On the stroke of noon on June 5, 1916, the nine black-robed men walked in, the chief justice and eight associate justices walking slowly down the aisle toward the front of the Senate Building's courtroom.

The chatter and whispering of the spectators died away as the line of men reached them. Those fortunate enough to have aisle seats thought they noticed a slight tremor in the hand of the last justice, the tall, fine-featured one who was carrying a Bible. No wonder he was nervous. . . . The whole country had been talking about him for months.

Louis was well aware that all eyes were on him. He was most of all conscious that he was wearing his new black silk robes for the first time. This was the uniform which would from now on mark him as a guardian of the United States Constitution to which he had just sworn allegiance in a private ceremony before his fellow justices.

The chief justice arranged himself on the podium. The other justices were seated. Louis stood, his back to the audience.

Somewhere in the visitor's gallery Alice, Susan and Elizabeth, his brother, Alfred, and a large group of friends were seated. Louis kept his eyes on the chief justice.

It was the gold medal presentation at the old high school in Louisville which flashed through his mind. The crowded auditorium . . . and there, near the front, proud and smiling, had been Adolph and Frederika Brandeis, his parents, who had come to see him honored. How he wished they could have had *this* moment.

One other he missed sadly today. Dear Sam Warren would have liked to see his prophecy come true. Sam was so sure his friend would reach the Supreme Court someday. What a pleasure it would be to say to him now, "Thanks, old friend, for believing in me."

How fortunate he was to have so many who believed in him. Would he ever forget the glistening in Alice's eyes and the lilt in her voice as she met him in their doorway after news of the Senate vote had reached her?

"Good evening, Mr. Justice Brandeis," she had welcomed him, and there, suddenly, the months of the ordeal had melted away for them both. The struggle was over. His fight had ended in victory.

There was no bitterness over the months just past. The many poisonous attacks upon his name would be washed away by the waves of time. The greatest challenge was still ahead. He had taken a few steps to lead the way. He knew best that it was only a beginning.

One of the justices held out the open Bible to him. Louis placed his left hand on it and slowly raised his right arm for his oath of office.

"I Louis Dembitz Brandeis, do solemnly swear that I will administer justice without respect to persons, and do equal right to the poor and to the rich, and that I will faithfully and impartially discharge and perform all the duties incumbent upon me as associate justice of the Supreme Court of the United States, according to the best of my abilities and understanding, agreeable to the Constitution and the laws of the United States. So help me God."

The following works have been of immeasurable help to me:

Brandeis: A Free Man's Life. Alpheus Thomas Mason. New York: Viking Press, 1956.

Justice on Trial: The Case of Louis D. Brandeis. A. L. Todd. New York: McGraw-Hill, 1964.

Louis D. Brandeis. Jacob de Haas. New York: Bloch, 1929.

I Remember. Abraham Flexner. New York: Simon and Schuster, 1940.

"Brandeis and the American Jewish Congress." C. Bezalel Sherman, in *Jewish Frontier*, June 1967.

Woodrow Wilson: A Great Life in Brief. John A. Garraty. New York: Alfred A. Knopf, 1956.

Woodrow Wilson: A Brief Biography. Arthur S. Link. Cleveland: World, 1963.

The Woodrow Wilson Story: An Idealist in Politics. Catherine Owens Peare. New York: Crowell, 1963.

Challenging Years: The Autobiography of Stephen S. Wise. New York: G. P. Putnam's Sons, 1949.